JOB SUCCESS

New Readers Press
ProLiteracy's publishing division

Job Success
ISBN 978-1-56420-497-4

Copyright ©2013
New Readers Press
ProLiteracy's Publishing Division
104 Marcellus Street, Syracuse, New York 13204
www.newreaderspress.com

adapted by permission from
Career Pathways: Effective Employee
Copyright ©2011
Paxen Learning Corporation

Printed in the United States of America
10   9   8   7   6   5   4   3

Proceeds from the sale of New Readers Press materials support professional
development, training, and technical assistance programs of ProLiteracy
that benefit local literacy programs in the U.S. and around the globe.

Image Credits:
Image on page 29 (GIS map) courtesy of The South Carolina Geological Survey
Image on page 26 (handheld police equipment) courtesy of Trimble Navigation Limited
Images on pages 41, 53, 54 ©Paxen Learning Corporation
Images on pages 11, 30, 33, 47, 59, 102, 109 iStockphoto
All other images Thinkstock

Editor: Gail Terp
Editorial Director: Terrie Lipke
Associate Director of Marketing and Communications: James P. Wallace
Technology Specialist: Maryellen Casey
Designer: Carolyn Wallace

Contents

CHAPTER 1: Starting Off

CHAPTER 2: Workplace Skills

CHAPTER 3: Job Performance

CHAPTER 4: Success on the Job

About this Book

Are you looking for a new job? Are you thinking about choosing a new career? Are you working to get a promotion or a better job? No matter where you are in your career, *Job Success* will help you prepare to succeed in today's workplace.

Here are some things to look for in this book. Every chapter includes GOALS, TERMS, and ACTIVITIES:

GOALS	Every lesson lists goals that tell you what you will learn.
TERMS	New vocabulary words are defined for each lesson.
ACTIVITIES	Answer questions, role-play work scenes, and practice reading work documents.

Other features focus on topics you should know about, such as:

JOB LAW	Understanding rules and laws about work
JOB TALK	Communicating with co-workers and supervisors
JOB TEAM	Working as part of a team
JOB TECH	Using technology at work
JOB & LIFE SKILLS	Balancing work and home life

Each chapter ends with a CHAPTER REVIEW. You will revisit your goals for the chapter and check your understanding of key terms and concepts.

At the end of the book, you will find a glossary and an answer key.

GLOSSARY	Practice your vocabulary with this list of terms and their definitions.
ANSWER KEY	You can check your own work on activities and reviews. Keep track of how much you have learned!

Before You Begin

When you start a new job, you bring all of your past experiences with you. You may have had other jobs. You may have done volunteer work. You may even have experience working for yourself, such as babysitting, fixing cars, or mowing lawns.

Before you begin this book, think about what experiences you have had in the past and what your job goals are for the future.

▶ What job would you like to have?

_____

_____

▶ What experience do you already have that may help you?

_____

_____

▶ What are you willing to do to prepare for this job?

_____

_____

▶ What do you like best about this job?

_____

_____

▶ What scares you about this job?

_____

_____

▶ What are your goals for this job and for your career?

_____

_____

A new job gives you a chance for a fresh start. Even if you have had bad experiences in the past, think positive about your goals for the future. A new job gives you the chance to learn from your negative experiences and build on your positive experiences.

Now you are on your way to *Job Success!*

Your New Job

GOALS

▶ LEARN about starting a new job

▶ LEARN about pay and deductions

▶ READ work schedules

TERMS

certificate a document that proves that you have trained for a skill

wage the amount of money a worker is paid

gross pay your pay before taxes and deductions are taken out

payroll deductions money taken from your paycheck for things like retirement savings and health insurance

net pay your pay after taxes and deductions are taken out

shift the time you are scheduled to work

For three months Antonio Garza searched for a job. Then he found one in an auto parts center. The center ships car parts all over the world. At first, Antonio was excited about his new job. But as he got closer to his first day, he began to have questions:

▶ How will I find my way around?
▶ Will I get along with the other workers?
▶ Will my boss see that I'm nervous?

Antonio thought a lot about these questions. He started to feel nervous. You may be like Antonio. You may also be nervous when starting a new job. Don't worry. The information in this chapter will teach you what you need to know. You will learn answers to your questions and do well in your new job.

Your First Day

You may be nervous or excited about starting your new job. But chances are you will do little real work on your first day. Most new employees (workers) spend their first day filling out paperwork. They may also be meeting their co-workers or going to training classes.

See the chart below for some of the forms you may need to fill out.

PAPERWORK FOR NEW EMPLOYEES

Paperwork	Explanation	Who Completes
W-4 Form	You need to put information about your family and your finances on this form. It tells the government how much to take out of your paycheck for taxes.	All employees
I-9 form	This form states that an employee can legally work in the United States. You will need your driver's license and Social Security card so that you and your employer can fill out this form. If you have a green card, you will need that too.	All employees
Direct deposit form	This form allows your employer to deposit your paycheck directly into your bank account. You will need the name of your bank and your account number.	Many employees who get a regular paycheck
Employee parking pass	This pass lets you park in an employer's parking lot. You may need to fill in the make, model, and license plate number of your car.	Employees who work in areas with limited parking
ID card	This card or badge will often have your name and photo. It may also show your identification number and the department in which you work.	Employees of companies that need safety
Certification	Some jobs require you to take a class or exam. When you pass, you get a **certificate.** You will need this certificate to show you have the right training for the job.	Many employees working in food service or health fields

Employee badges sometimes have bar codes or magnetic strips.

ACME

EMPLOYEE

Antonio Garza
ID: 00213

Wages and Pay

A **wage** is the amount of money a worker is paid. Wages are also called pay. How you are paid depends on the type of job you have. You may be paid a set salary or by the hour. If you are paid a salary, you get the same amount of money each pay period. A pay period is usually one week, two weeks, or one month. If you are paid by the hour, you are paid just for the number of hours you work in a pay period.

Gross pay is your pay *before* taxes and any other payroll deductions are taken out. **Payroll deductions** take money from your paycheck for things like retirement savings and health insurance.

Net pay is your pay *after* taxes and other deductions are taken out. Net pay is also called take-home pay.

If you are paid by the hour, you may earn extra pay for working on holidays. You may also earn extra pay if you work more than 40 hours a week. This is called overtime.

Income tax is money paid to the government. This money is withheld (subtracted) from your pay. Federal income tax is paid to the U.S. government. State income tax is paid to your state.

The amount of income tax taken from your paycheck varies. Income tax is based on the number of dependents you claim on your W-4 form. Your dependents are people who rely on you for financial support. This could be your wife or husband, your children, or other family members.

For each dependent you claim, the government withholds less money from your paycheck. This means you will get more take-home pay. Suppose you earned $600 gross pay a week. If you claim no dependents, $33.00 will be withheld. If you claim one dependent, $7.17 will be withheld.

The more dependents you claim, the more pay you will take home. But when you file your income taxes in April, you may get a smaller tax refund or even have to pay taxes. You must choose whether you need more money in each paycheck or you would like a larger yearly tax refund.

For example, let's say you make $9.50 an hour, and you work 35 hours per week. Your gross pay is $332.50. After federal and state taxes are deducted, you may get only about $275.00. If you have other deductions, such as health care or savings, you may take home even less.

JOB MATH

A calculator is really helpful for this.

Figure Out Your Gross Wages

How do you figure out gross pay? Multiply your weekly wage by 52 to get your yearly pay. Now practice your job math.

1. Kiri earns $10.00 an hour. She works 40 hours each week. How much does Kiri earn?

	Weekly	Every 2 Weeks	Yearly
	10.00 × 40 Wage × hours	10.00 × 40 × 2 Wage × hours × 2	10.00 × 40 × 52 Wage × hours × weeks
Gross Pay			

2. Jeff earns $11.65 an hour. He works 30 hours each week. How much does Jeff earn?

	Weekly	Every 2 Weeks	Yearly
	11.65 × 30 Wage × hours	11.65 × 30 × 2 Wage × hours × 2	11.65 × 30 × 52 Wage × hours × weeks
Gross Pay			

Learn Your Way Around

Many employers give new employees a tour of their workplace. But if this does not happen, be sure to ask questions. Try to get maps or floor plans to find important places at your new job.

See the example of a workplace floor plan below.

Follow the directions to mark certain areas on the floor plan.

1. The warehouse is on the left side of the floor plan. Circle one of the yellow forklifts.

2. Make an *X* in the reception area. The reception area is the place visitors go when they walk in the front door. The reception area is on the right side of the floor plan, northeast of the warehouse. It has a red couch. There is usually a person working in the reception area who greets visitors.

3. Make a pound sign (#) in the conference room. The conference room is on the right side of the floor plan, northwest of the reception area. Use the compass rose to help you find it.

4. Make a star (★) in the technology work area. It is in the middle of the floor plan, north of the warehouse. It is near the fire exit. Do you see the fire exit?

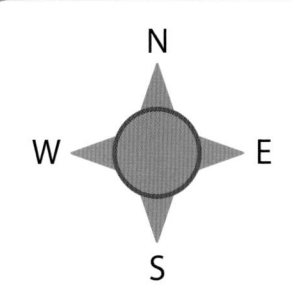

This symbol is called a compass rose. It is used to show north, south, east, and west. The letters N, S, E, and W stand for the directions.

← LEFT

RIGHT →

Understanding Work Schedules

A work schedule tells you what days you are working and at what times. Some employees work the same schedule week after week. Others have schedules that change. As a new employee, it is important that you learn how to read and understand your work schedule. Supervisors usually make these schedules ahead of time. They may hand out copies of the schedule or post it where everyone can see.

Once you know your schedule, you can plan events in your own life around your work. Some supervisors may let you trade **shifts** with your co-workers if you need time off. But not all will allow this. Be sure to ask your supervisor if you need to make any changes to your schedule.

It is important you follow your work schedule carefully. This is true if you are new and if you have worked at a place for a long time. This shows you are a dependable employee—someone your employer can trust.

A good tip: always be sure you are reading from the correct week's schedule. And when you start a new job, ask your supervisor if you have any questions about your schedule.

Activity

Read Work Schedules

This schedule shows one way a company may schedule work. Read the schedule. Then answer the questions.

WORK SCHEDULE APRIL 5–11							
NAME	MON	TUES	WED	THURS	FRI	SAT	SUN
Olivia	8am-4pm				8am-4pm	10am-3pm	
Reynaldo	4pm-10pm	4pm-7pm	4pm-10pm		4pm-7pm		10am-3pm
Hanh		8am-4pm		4pm-10pm			
Ashley		7pm-10pm		8am-4pm	7pm-10pm		
Skylar	8am-11am	8am-11am	8am-11am	8am-11am	8am-11am		

1. How many total hours does Olivia work during this week?
   _____

2. Which employee begins work immediately after Ashley's shift on Thursday?
   _____

3. Which employee works only pm shifts Monday through Friday?
   _____

4. Who works alone on Saturday? _____

5. What hours does Ashley work on Friday? _____

6. What is the longest shift that anyone works this week?
   _____

7. Who works only morning hours? _____

8. What week is this schedule for? _____

Math Tip: There are two ways to work out how long a shift is:

1. If the times are both either am or pm, subtract the beginning time from the end time.
   Example: 4pm-10pm 10 – 4 = 6. This is a 6-hour shift.

2. If the times are am and pm, count up the hours from the beginning time to the end time.
   Example: 8am-4pm Count up from 8: 9-10-11-12-1-2-3-4. This is an 8-hour shift.

Know Your Rights

There are federal, state, and local laws that protect your rights at work. This table explains how these laws apply to break times and overtime pay. Many companies give breaks to their employees, even if the law does not require it.

Federal	The Fair Labor Standards Act (FLSA) controls overtime pay. It guarantees (promises) overtime pay to hourly employees. Pay must be at least time-and-a-half for overtime work. That means 1.5 times your regular rate of pay. Workers who get a regular salary are not guaranteed overtime pay. There is no federal law that says workers must get breaks.
State	Eight states require employers to offer paid breaks to employees. Some states provide extra overtime protections for employees.

Sharing your lunch break with co-workers can give you a chance to get to know them better. Friendly co-workers are more likely to support one another on the job.

Workplace Policies

Chapter ①

GOALS

▶ LEARN how company rules affect you

▶ READ parts of two policy manuals

▶ ROLE PLAY how to talk to your boss

TERMS

policies the rules a company makes to keep work going well and safely

conduct the way you behave; your behavior

harassment conduct meant to disturb or upset another employee

discrimination unfair treatment of a person or group of people

You have started your new job–great! But now you may have even more questions. You may wonder, "Who should I call if I am sick?" Or you may wonder, "What should I do if I get hurt at work?" Luckily, your company has a policy manual to answer these questions. **Policies** are the rules a company makes to keep work going well and safely. The policy manual lists and explains them. Following policies can help you succeed on the job.

A policy manual can tell you a lot. By reading it, you can learn:

▶ How the company is organized
▶ Rules for employee **conduct**
▶ Compensation (how workers get paid)
▶ Guidelines for use of company property

You should get a copy of the policy manual as soon as you begin your new job. See the sample policy manual table of contents on page 13. It explains how this information may be presented.

This part tells about the company and how it is organized or set up. It also gives information about things such as
- employee responsibilities
- how to work out conflicts
- ways to get ahead in your job

This part describes
- working hours and schedules
- how to clock in and out of work
- how to call in sick and take vacation time

Midwest
WINDOWS AND DOORS

COMPANY POLICY MANUAL

This part explains the
- dress code
- drug and alcohol policies
- rules about weapons and violence
- rules about conduct or how you should behave at work

This part gives
- rules for using company equipment
- safety rules for using company vehicles or machinery

This part has information such as
- pay and pay periods
- deductions
- expense reports
- employee benefits (such as health insurance and retirement plans)

You are responsible for following all policies. It is important to read each page carefully. Ask questions if there is something you do not understand. You can ask your supervisor or the human resources (HR) manager.

EMPLOYEE CONDUCT

A policy manual is split into sections. The employee conduct section is one of the most important. It will help you know how to behave at work. It will tell what you should wear to work. It will tell how you should act and what behaviors are not allowed.

Every workplace has rules that protect employees. Some protect against harassment and discrimination. **Harassment** is conduct meant to upset or threaten another employee. **Discrimination** is unfair treatment of a person or group of people. This may be made on the basis of race or religion. You must follow all policies, so read each page carefully.

Dress Code

A dress code tells what you should wear to work. There are three common workplace dress codes. These are uniform, business, and casual. The easiest to follow is the uniform dress code. It lists exactly what you should wear. Your employer may even give you a uniform.

Business dress codes can vary from workplace to workplace. Sometimes men are expected to wear a suit or tie. Sometimes they are not. Women often have more choices. Look at what other employees are wearing. This is a good way to tell what is OK to wear.

With a casual dress code, you may be able to wear jeans and T-shirts. But you should never wear dirty or ripped clothing. You should not wear T-shirts with comments or sayings.

Activity

Understand Workplace Policies

Here are examples from a policy manual. Use this information to answer the questions below.

1. Could an employee who has a legal gun permit bring a gun to work?

2. Give 3 examples of conduct that might be considered harassment.

3. Jamal begins a full-time job at this company on September 1. How many days of vacation pay will he have by the end of the year?

Uniform   Business Casual   Casual Dress

SPEEDY Delivery Services

Company Policy Manual

Prohibited (banned) on company property:

• Possession, use, or sale of drugs and alcoholic beverages

• Possession or use of firearms or explosives

Harassment can be defined as hostile (negative) conduct toward someone that affects that person's work performance. There shall be no conduct that creates an intimidating or hostile work environment.

Full-time employees will immediately begin adding vacation pay at a rate of one day per month. Employees can earn up to 10 days per year. Up to five unused vacation days can be used in the next year.

Sometimes a dress code will be very detailed. Other times you will need to use your best judgment to decide what to wear to work.

Working With Your Supervisor

Your supervisor is the best person to ask for work information. She can answer your work policy questions. Your supervisor may also correct you if you break the rules, such as not wearing your uniform.

Your supervisor can be your most important co-worker. Workers who have strong relationships with their bosses can go far in a company. Those who don't often do not do as well. This means it's a good idea to get to know your supervisor and her working style.

Watch your supervisor's style of management. Watch how she acts with employees. Does your supervisor act formally? Or does she seem friendly and casual? Do workers call her by her first name, or by a title such as Mrs. or Ms.?

Match your communication style to your supervisor's. For example, if your supervisor seems casual, it may be OK to make suggestions in person. If your supervisor is more formal, you may need to put your comments in writing.

Activity

Communication Role Play

Here is a conversation between a boss and his employee. The employee (Beth) calls her boss to say she is sick and cannot come to work. Note that Beth tells what's wrong but does not give too many details of her illness.

Boss: Hello?

Employee: Hello, Mr. Thomas. This is Beth Jackson.

Boss: Hello, Beth. What can I do for you?

Employee: I'm sorry, Mr. Thomas. I'm not feeling well. I felt like I was coming down with the flu last night. This morning it's worse. I don't want to get anyone else sick, so I'm going to stay home. I hope this won't be a problem.

Boss: No, that's fine. You just stay home and get better. Call me tomorrow if you are still sick. I hope you feel better soon.

Employee: Thank you. I hope so too! Goodbye.

Boss: Goodbye.

Your Turn

Work with a classmate on this activity. You will practice talking as an employee and a supervisor. For each situation, take turns so you can practice both parts.

1. An employee calls his supervisor to explain that he has car trouble and will be late to work. (Be honest. Everyone has been in this situation. If you can, say when you will arrive.)

2. An employee speaks to her supervisor to request a day off. (Depending on company policy, you may not have to explain why you want a day off. Sometimes it helps to say why, if it's for a special event.)

3. A supervisor asks an employee to work overtime. The employee must get home to take care of his children. The employee respectfully declines and says he would be happy to work overtime another time if he has more notice.

Procedures and Benefits

GOALS

▶ PRACTICE reading procedure manuals

▶ LEARN how company benefits affect you

▶ COMPARE two benefit packages

TERMS

procedure the steps you follow in order to do something.

human resources the department in a company that deals with hiring, training, and other employee issues

coverage the amount or type of protection given by an insurance plan

deductible the amount you must pay before insurance begins to cover your expenses

co-pay payment you must make each time you get medical care

Lesson 2 talked about policy manuals. Some companies also have procedure manuals. A **procedure** manual gives you step-by-step instructions for doing important tasks. For example, you may need to learn how to safely use a machine. Or you might need to learn about food safety rules in a restaurant. If you have a technical job, you may have a procedure manual for each task you do. See the example below to learn more.

> Procedure manuals are usually split into parts. Each part tells about a different job task.

AXIS CHEMICALS

Hazardous Chemical Containers

Employees must label all containers of dangerous chemicals. These labels should include

- the name of the chemical
- a warning
- the name and address of the chemical manufacturer (maker)

> Step-by-step directions tell how to do important tasks. They explain how to safely handle hazardous or dangerous chemicals.

If the label can't be read or is missing, employees must find or make a label. See the supervisor to get blank labels.

Employees working with hazardous chemicals that run through pipes must contact their supervisor to get the following information:

1. names of the chemicals
2. possible health risks of these chemicals
3. safety steps and safety equipment needed

> Procedure manuals can also tell employees where to find more information or who to contact for more help.

Learning Procedures

Procedure manuals come in different sizes. Some might be only a few pages. Others could be very long. No matter the size, take your time when reading your manual. Read it carefully and make sure you understand it. If you are not sure about a procedure, ask. Your supervisor can explain it further.

Your procedure manual may cover many things. It may cover safety procedures, such as wearing protective gear. It may tell you what to do in an emergency, such as a fire.

Your procedure manual may also help you handle tasks such as filing a grievance. A grievance is a written complaint. You might wish to file a grievance if you feel that someone has harassed you or treated you unfairly. You may need to fill out forms and your manual can help with that.

Your procedure manual will tell you what to do if you need to call in sick. You may need to call your supervisor or a **human resources** (HR) manager when you are ill. You may need to have a doctor's note when you return to work.

The Family and Medical Leave Act (FMLA) is a law. It allows employees to get unpaid time off for certain family and health issues. It covers things such as pregnancy, child care, and adoption. It also covers workers who have serious health problems or who must care for sick family members. FMLA now covers other people, such as grandparents, who care for children. Your manual will tell you how to apply for FMLA time off.

Both men and women can use FMLA to care for newborn or adopted children.

JOB LAW

FAMILY AND MEDICAL LEAVE ACT (FMLA)

Reasons that qualify for leave	Pregnancy, prenatal medical care, or childbirth
	To care for the employee's child after birth, or placement for adoption or foster care
	To care for the employee's spouse, son, daughter, or parent with a serious health condition
	A serious health condition that makes the employee unable to perform his or her job
	Some situations in military families
Limits and protections	12 weeks of unpaid leave
	Employee is guaranteed job when he or she returns
	Health care coverage is maintained
	Employees return to their original or equal jobs at the same pay and benefits
Employee/ employer requirements	Employee has worked for the employer for at least one year
	Employee has worked for at least 1,250 hours over the previous 12 months
	Employer has at least 50 employees
Employee responsibilities	Provide 30 days advance notice (when possible)
	When 30 days' notice is not possible, must provide notice as soon as possible. Provide needed information for the employer to decide if the employee qualifies for FMLA leave
	Must give the time and length of the leave
Employer responsibilities	Inform employees whether they qualify for an FMLA leave
	If they do not qualify, the employer must provide a reason

Employee Benefits

As an employee, you receive wages (pay) for the work that you do. You may also get other benefits from your employer. Benefits are things like health care plans and paid vacation. This table explains some common benefits.

With some jobs, you may get other benefits. Food service workers often get free or low-cost meals during breaks. Employees of cell phone companies may get free phones. Store clerks often get an employee discount. This allows them to buy clothing or other store goods at a lower price.

Employers give these benefits so that workers know about products the company offers. Workers can then tell the customers. Have you ever asked a waiter in a restaurant about a dish? He may know what he is talking about because he had a chance to try the food for free.

Be sure to ask what benefits are available to you.

DIRECT BENEFITS

Benefit	Description
Paid vacation days	Employees get a certain number of days that they can use for vacation. They get paid for these days.
Health care benefits	These often include health insurance for employees and their families. Companies may pay for all or part of a health insurance plan.
Retirement plans	These plans allow employees to put some of their wages into a retirement account. Income tax is not withheld from this money.
Child care	Employers provide a child care center for the children of employees during work hours.
Tuition reimbursement	Employers help pay for employees to take classes or to get more training for their jobs.
Profit sharing	An employer splits some of its profits among employees.

Health Care

More than half of all workers in the U.S. have some type of health care plan through their employers. There are many different types of plans. When you begin a job, you will learn about the plans available to you. The human resources staff can tell you about the plan. They can also help you figure out the best choice for you.

When comparing health care plans, you should always look at the types of coverage these plans give. **Coverage** is the amount or type of protection given by an insurance plan. Some plans may only offer basic medical coverage. Others may cover vision and dental care, as well.

Pay attention to the deductibles. **Deductibles** are the amounts you must pay before insurance begins to cover your expenses.

It is important to choose the best possible plan for you. The best plan may not be the cheapest. Co-pays may also affect which plan you choose. A **co-pay** is a payment you must make each time you get medical care.

At times, you may need to change your health benefits or coverage. Marriage, divorce, or childbirth can affect the type of benefits you need. Your employer should let you know how to make any changes. If you change jobs or lose your job, you may also be able to buy health coverage through your former employer's plan.

Activity

Health Care Plan A or B?

Work with a partner. Review the two health care plans shown here. Then decide which plan would work best for you. When you have made your choice, write which plan you chose and list the reasons you chose it.

Health Care Plan A
- Monthly Employee Cost
  ◦ $151.56 (Individual)
  ◦ $444.30 (Family)
- Benefits
  ◦ medical
  ◦ maternity
  ◦ hospital
- Co-pay:
  $20 for doctor visits and prescription drugs
- Employees can visit doctors of their choice
- Annual deductible: $0

Health Care Plan B
- Monthly Employee Cost
  ◦ $145.36 (Individual)
  ◦ $402.60 (Family)
- Benefits
  ◦ medical
  ◦ maternity
  ◦ hospital
- Co-pay:
  $40 for doctor visits and prescription drugs
- Employees can only visit doctors in the plan's network
- Annual deductible: $500

> *Most health care plans cover prescription medications. That means they pay for part or all of the medicine your doctor prescribes.*

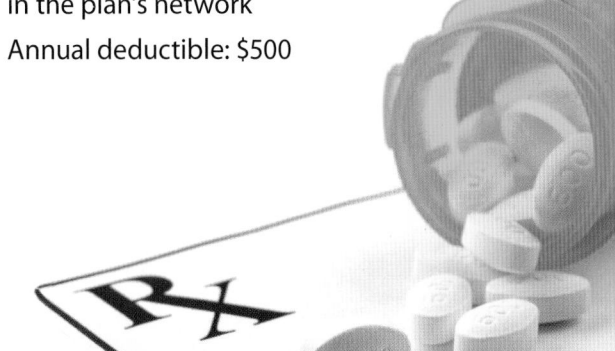

Learning Your Job

GOALS

▶ PREPARE to do your job well

▶ PRACTICE reading training manuals and safety warnings

▶ LEARN how to work with a mentor

TERMS

mentor a more experienced employee who helps train a new worker

technology the use of science to solve problems or invent useful things; sometimes called *tech*

lingo the special terms used by a group of people

hazard danger; something that can cause harm

Ben Davis arrived for his first day of work at The French Café. Ben had trained as a chef at his local college. But this was his first time in a restaurant kitchen. Ben was nervous and had questions:

▶ Will they like how I cook?
▶ Will I know how to use all the equipment?
▶ What if they ask me to cook something I don't know how to make?

Ben did not need to worry. Like most employers, The French Café trains all its new employees. In the first few weeks, Ben will be trained in all the kitchen equipment and procedures.

Employers train new workers to teach them the skills they need for their jobs. Training might include learning how to use a computer program or how to use special tools.

Training is not just for the new workers. When there is new equipment, all workers need to be trained. In some jobs, new training happens all the time.

In some jobs, such as plumbing or carpentry, new employees may begin as apprentices. Apprentices work for others in order to learn a job. They can move to higher levels as they become more skilled.

COMMON TYPES OF TRAINING

Industry	Training Manual	Video Training	Working with a Mentor	Apprenticeship
Health care	X	X	X	X
Food service/stores	X	X	X	
Technology	X	X		
Skilled trades	X		X	X

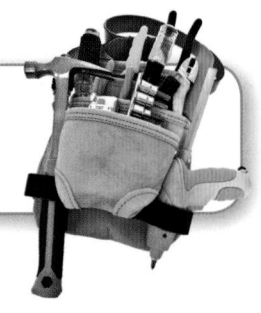

An apprentice learns new job skills by working with an experienced employee.

Formal Training

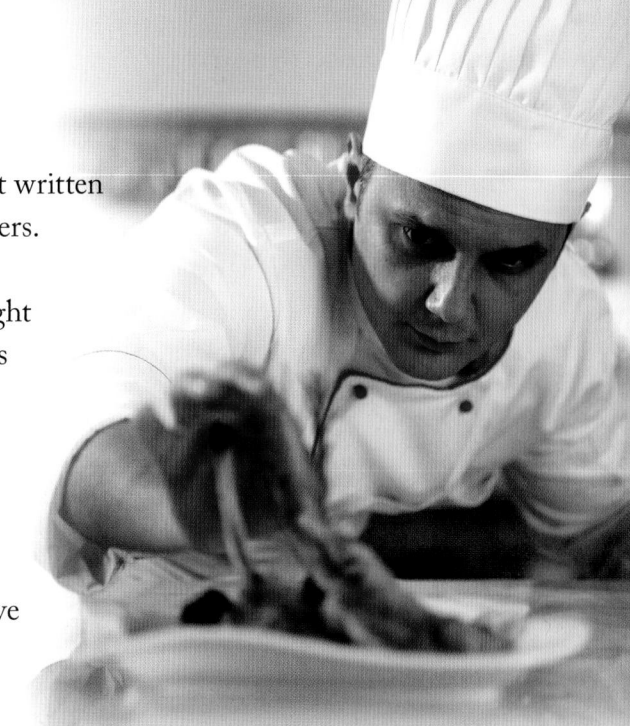

Employers train their employees in different ways. Some give out written training manuals. Others use longtime employees to train new workers. Often, employers mix formal and informal types of training.

Formal training is more organized than informal training. It might be held in a training center, a classroom, or at work. Some training is followed by a test. This shows your employer that you have learned the skills you need to do your job.

As a new employee, you should take an active role in your training. Make sure you have the right manual. Find out which person to go to when you have questions. It's a good idea to take notes during your training. Notes will help you remember what you've learned. Ask how to get more training if you think you need it.

Activity

Understand Training Manuals

Read this section from a Security Guard Training Manual. Next, write three questions about this manual on the lines below. Ask your questions aloud and discuss the answers in class.

SECURITY GUARD
TRAINING MANUAL

STAY ALERT * LISTEN * LOOK

If a problem should occur, follow these instructions:

1. Do not approach the offender.

2. Remain calm. Watch what is happening.

3. Write down what you see as soon as possible. This will help you remember what happened.

4. Report what happened to the police.

5. Report what happened to your supervisor.

1. _____

   _____

   _____

2. _____

   _____

   _____

3. _____

   _____

   _____

Workplace Safety

In your work, you will likely see safety warning signs like those seen below. These signs warn you about a nearby hazard. A **hazard** is a danger or risk. The signs may also tell you how to stay safe.

You can recognize many safety signs by their symbols or pictures. For instance, a picture of a person slipping and falling means a wet floor. These symbols and pictures help people to quickly understand what the signs mean, even if they can't read the words.

You should learn the safety signs used at your work. Follow the signs' warnings, to help keep work safe for you and others.

Some safety warnings are found on labels. A container may have a warning label. A piece of equipment may also have one. These labels tell you how to use products or equipment safely. Warning labels often have more information than warning signs.

Activity

Safety Warnings

Study the signs and the information below. Then answer the question that follows.

Construction workers might see this sign. It warns about nearby electrical wires. Workers should not dig where power lines are buried.

This sign tells you to wear goggles to protect your eyes. Scientists, firefighters, or metal workers might see these signs.

This sign tells you that a floor is wet. Workers on cleaning crews often use these signs. You may see them in public places.

This sign warns you that a product is dangerous. Some workers use poisons, such as pest control or cleaning products.

What types of warning signs have you seen?

_____

_____

_____

_____

_____

_____

_____

_____

_____

_____

_____

_____

_____

Protect Yourself

Wearing proper safety gear helps keep you safe on the job. It is also your responsibility.

Safety gear includes things like this:

- hard hats
- gloves
- face shields
- dust masks
- earplugs
- rubber boots

The law says employers must provide you with the safety gear you need. If your company does not provide it, it can get in trouble with the law.

If you do not wear your safety gear, you can get in trouble, too. Suppose you did not wear your safety gear one day, and you got hurt. You could be held responsible for your injury. You might have to pay the medical bills. Your employer would not be responsible for them.

Study this photo. Notice where the workers are and the safety gear they are wearing. What type of work do you think these people are doing?

Informal Training

On page 21, you learned about formal training for new employees. Your new job may include informal training.

One common type of informal training is to work with a mentor. **Mentors** are more experienced employees who help train new workers. Mentors can help by answering questions. They can give advice. They can tell new workers things they may not learn in their formal training.

At times, you may work with a mentor who does not behave appropriately. He might speak poorly of the company, your boss, or another co-worker. If this happens, ignore this talk. Instead, form your own opinions. It is best to focus on the positive advice your mentor gives.

JOB TALK

Communication Styles

In your job, you may work with people who have different ways of communicating. One may speak very fast. Another may speak with a strong accent. Some may stand too close. Others may not talk much at all.

It can be hard to communicate with someone whose style is not like your own. You may have to ask a co-worker to repeat something he said too quickly. Or, if a co-worker stands too close, you may need to ask her to give you more space.

To succeed in your job, you need to be able to communicate well. The key is to be polite and respectful. This will help you share your thoughts and feelings. It will also help avoid conflict.

Many companies use mentoring. It is a great way to develop effective employees.

Workplace Lingo

Every business has its own lingo. **Lingo** is the special language used by a group of people. When you start a new job, you may not know its lingo. But your co-workers may use it all the time. And they may not know you aren't familiar with it. Ask other workers to explain words you don't understand. Try to remember them. That way, you can begin using them in your work, too.

Your mentor can be a great help when it comes to learning lingo. Some new people feel embarrassed to ask co-workers about words they don't understand. But if you have a good relationship with your mentor, you may feel more comfortable asking him to explain.

JOB TALK

Learn the Lingo

Below are some examples of lingo from different jobs.

Health Care

a.c. before meals

appy a person's appendix or a patient with appendicitis

bounceback a patient who returns with the same complaints shortly after being released from the hospital

CBC complete blood count; a blood test that is used to diagnose different illnesses

ICU intensive care unit

stat immediately; right away

tox screen blood test for drugs in a patient's system

Retail

brick and mortar a store located in a building, rather than on a website or in a temporary location

comp sales a measure used to compare sales income in similar type stores

cross sell a sales approach in which a salesperson suggests another item to buy; for instance, recommending a scarf to go along with a new coat

sales floor the section of the store where products are displayed and sold

SKU stock keeping unit; a number given to each item for sale that is used to track information about that item

Manufacturing

backlog a build-up of tasks that have not been completed

batch a set of items produced through a single process

plant a factory or workshop at which products are manufactured

prototype an original item from which additional copies are made

quality control a process that reviews the quality of products

r&d research and development; a process to develop new products or systems, or to improve existing ones

Information Technology

Technology in the Workplace

Technology in the workplace helps you work faster, better, and smarter. **Technology** is the use of science to solve problems or invent useful things. Today, almost every job uses some type of technology. Store clerks use it to ring up sales. Truck drivers use a tracking computer to keep a record of their trips.

Sometimes technology can confuse and even scare new employees. But it is important to know how to use it. To do your job well, you may need to depend on it. For that reason, make sure that you get the training you need. Ask for and read the training books. Ask for more training if you feel you need it.

Technology is there to help you do your job. Read on to see how workers in different jobs use technology.

LAW ENFORCEMENT

People in law enforcement need to get information from many sources. It would be hard for them to carry books, maps, and report forms with them all the time. Instead, they use laptop computers and other devices to help them while on duty.

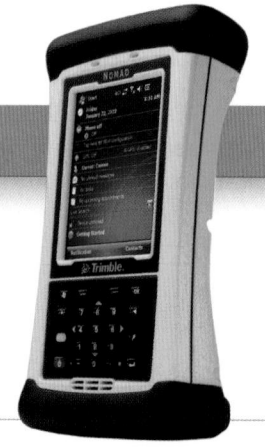

This mini-computer helps officers find information and file reports.

MEDICINE

Technology is used in doctors' offices and hospitals every day. Doctors use it to diagnose (identify) illness. Doctors also use it to check on and treat patients when they are ill.

New technology can do some amazing things. It can help people breathe when their lungs are not working well. It can clean blood and can even help a heart pump blood.

Technology can improve hospital care. It can lead to simpler treatment and shorter stays in the hospital. Technology helps make operations safer. And it helps patients heal faster.

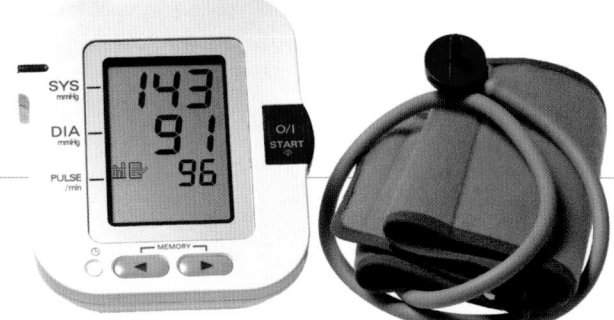

This blood pressure device lets health care staff measure blood pressure. It can also be used by patients themselves. Keeping track of changes in blood pressure is part of good health care.

Health care workers use technology to do many jobs, from taking temperatures to recording patient information.

Information Technology

TRUCKING

Truckers need to know where they are going. Many years ago, they used printed maps. Today, they use a global positioning system, or GPS. GPS devices give turn-by-turn directions to almost anywhere.

FARMING

Farmers now use computers in their tractors. It helps them steer their tractors. Plus, it helps them test the soil as they plow.

Activity

Use a GPS

Use a GPS device (or MapQuest or Google Maps) to plan a route:

- from your home to a friend's house
- from your home to a place where you have applied for a job

Analyze GIS Data

Natural resources, such as water, coal, and oil, can be found and mapped using GIS data. Such information can help government departments and businesses. The map below is of South Carolina. It shows some of the state's resources. Use the information on the map to answer the following questions.

1. Why might a jewelry maker be interested in this state?

2. Near which natural resource might a cement company want to build a factory?

3. Kaolin is used in making paper. Does this state seem to be a good place to get kaolin?

4. Fuller's earth is used to make kitty litter. Does this state have more fuller's earth or coquina?

Business People, Miners, Farmers, and Teachers

GIS also gives lots of useful information. GIS stands for Geographic Information System. It is a computer program that finds, stores, and shows information about the land. GIS can give us all kinds of information.

- GIS can show where people with high and low incomes live. This would be helpful for deciding where to build a new store.

- GIS can show where resources such as sand or gold are found. This would be helpful to miners or makers of cement.

- GIS can show changes in the land caused by weather. Teachers can use this information in their lessons.

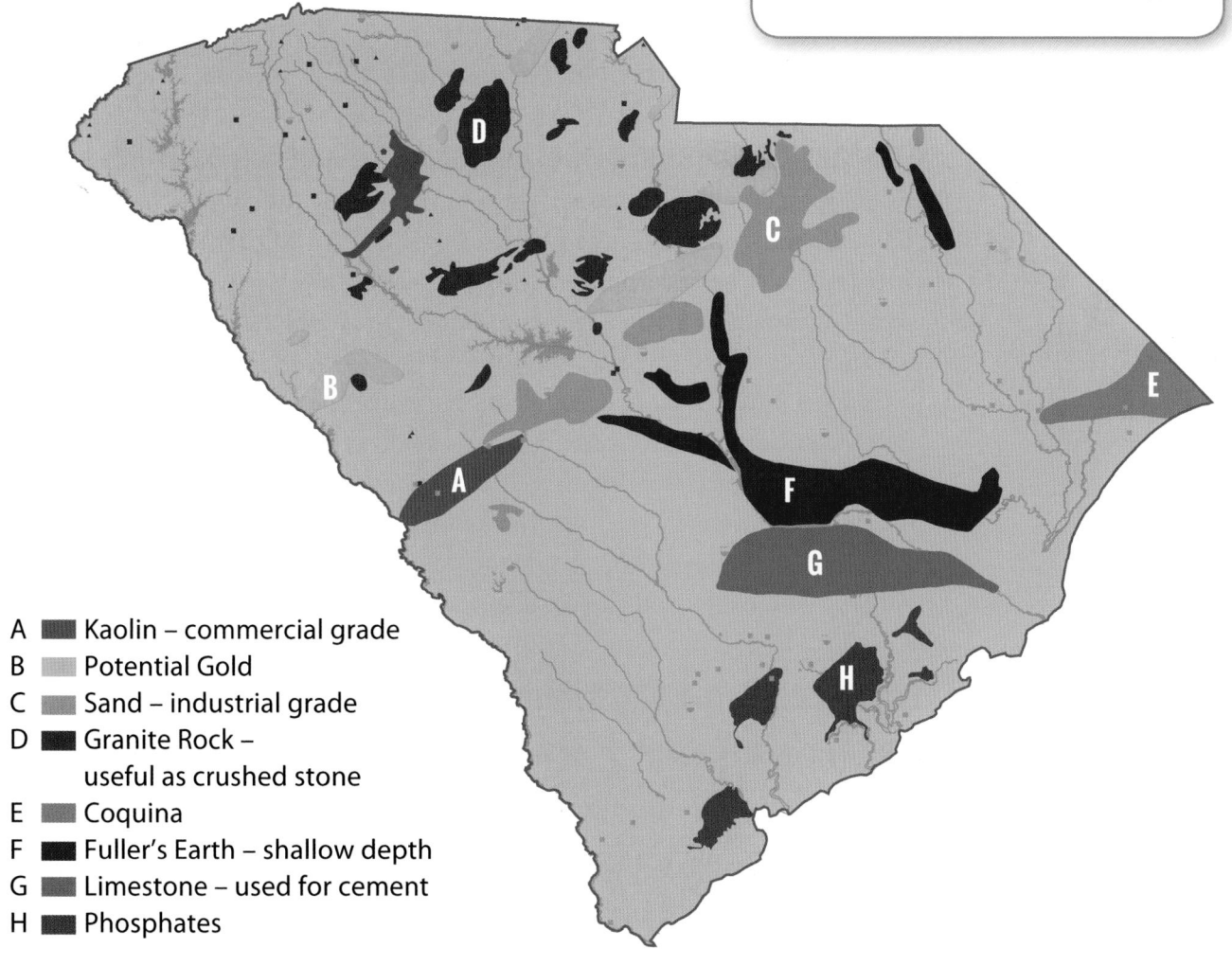

A ▰ Kaolin – commercial grade
B ▰ Potential Gold
C ▰ Sand – industrial grade
D ▰ Granite Rock – useful as crushed stone
E ▰ Coquina
F ▰ Fuller's Earth – shallow depth
G ▰ Limestone – used for cement
H ▰ Phosphates

Corporate Culture

GOALS

▶ LEARN how corporate culture affects you

▶ LEARN about networking and socializing at work

▶ THINK ABOUT how you can fit into the corporate culture

Terms

corporate culture the values and behavior of the people in a company

networking building relationships with other people to help your career

incentive something that encourages a person to work harder

Company manuals tell a lot of information about how a business is run.

But they don't tell it all. Instead, there are other clues all around you. Look at the values and behavior of the people in your company. They form its **corporate culture.** The rules of corporate culture are not usually written down. Often, they are not even talked about. Over time, employees watch how others act and learn to fit in.

Shauna Taylor is a cashier in a grocery store. She noticed that many of her co-workers wore football shirts to work on fall weekends. Her boss wore one, too. Shauna learned that wearing the shirts was part of her store's corporate culture. She decided she would wear one the following weekend.

As a new employee, you should look out for signs of corporate culture. This will help you make good choices about when and how to join in.

Examples of Corporate Culture

In some jobs, you may only display personal items, such as family pictures, in certain places.

The health care field has a strict code of behavior. Nurses often call each other by their first names. But a doctor is addressed as "Dr. Morse."

Large stores often give out prizes to employees who sell the most in a week or month.

Cultural Clues

Study the photos below. Then describe how each photo shows a clue about corporate culture.

A. _____

_____

_____

B. _____

_____

_____

C. _____

_____

_____

D. _____

_____

_____

Corporate Culture Affects Employees

Corporate culture sometimes includes things employers do to encourage workers to do their best. Some employers reward employees with incentives. An **incentive** is a gift that rewards an employee for working hard or for reaching a goal. Some companies give small gifts to good workers. Some might reward the whole staff with a party.

Tim Hicks is a manager for a call center. Tim needs his employees to handle a lot of calls and to make customers happy. He believes that the employees will do better work if they are happy too. To help his staff stay positive, he rewards them. He listens while they talk to customers. When he hears a worker being cheerful and helpful, he gives him a special card. The card is good for a free drink in the break room.

Some companies create sports teams for their workers. It may be a bowling or a softball team. Playing sports together helps build strong work relationships.

There are many ways a company can encourage employees to do their best work. It may be praise, a gift, parties, or team sports. The goal is the same—happy employees who do their best.

JOB LAW

Too Much of a Good Thing

Taking part in corporate culture can be both fun and rewarding. But you must not take it too far.

Do you get together with co-workers outside of work? Don't be tempted to behave in ways that would not be OK at work. Don't drink too much. Avoid inappropriate contact with co-workers. Remember that bad behavior with your co-workers can affect your job.

If you have a chance to use company extras, such as sports tickets or a gym, use them responsibly. If you use a company credit card, be careful to follow the rules. Remember, your actions can get you in trouble with your job and with the law.

Networking and Socializing

A good way to be part of the corporate culture at work is through networking. **Networking** is when you build relationships with other people that will help your career. There are many ways to network. Going to work-related events is a good way to meet new people.

Socializing or getting together with co-workers is another way to network. Joining co-workers in after-work events is a good way to get to know people in your company.

Suppose that once a month a group of office workers goes bowling. Douglas hates bowling, so he never goes. Sindi isn't good at bowling, but she knows that the point of the event is not to get the highest score. The point is to connect with her co-workers.

Often, Sindi bowls in the same lane with her supervisor, Nina. Nina sees how Sindi interacts with the others. She likes Sindi's good attitude. The next time Nina has a special project, she may think of asking Sindi.

Remember Shauna, who works at the grocery store that lets workers wear football shirts? Wearing one too shows that Shauna wants to be part of the team.

Activity

Where Do You Fit In?

Socializing with co-workers is a great way to network. It can be one of the fun parts of working. But there can be some drawbacks. While it is good to have fun, you still need to respect the rules of proper work conduct.

How might you fit in with the corporate culture at work? If you don't have a job, imagine yourself in the job that you want. Think about the following questions. Then discuss your answers with the class.

1. How could you learn about the corporate culture at your work?

2. What corporate culture activity would you feel comfortable being part of? Explain your choice.

3. What corporate culture activity would you not feel comfortable being part of? Explain your choice.

Chapter Review

Check off the goals you achieved in Chapter 1.

In Lesson 1, you . . .

☐ Learned about starting a new job

☐ Learned about pay and deductions

☐ Learned to read work schedules

In Lesson 2, you . . .

☐ Learned how company rules affect you

☐ Learned to read policy manuals

☐ Role-played how to talk to your boss

In Lesson 3, you . . .

☐ Practiced reading procedure manuals

☐ Learned how company benefits affect you

☐ Compared two benefits packages

In Lesson 4, you . . .

☐ Prepared to do your job well

☐ Practiced reading training manuals and safety warnings

☐ Learned how to work with a mentor

In Lesson 5, you . . .

☐ Learned how corporate culture affects you

☐ Learned about networking and socializing at work

☐ Thought about how you can fit into the corporate culture

What do you want to know more about? Write the things that you want to learn more about. Talk to your teacher or look them up online.

_____

_____

Choose the best answer.

1. What is the best way to find information about an employer's rules?

    A. look them up online

    B. read the company's policy manual

    C. call the company's office for information

    D. ask a co-worker for information

True or false? If the statement is true, write T. If the statement is false, write F. Then change the false statement to make it true.

2. For each dependent you claim on your W-4 form, the government withholds more money from your paycheck.

   _____

3. If a mentor speaks poorly about an employer or co-worker, you should ignore this talk and form your own conclusions.

   _____

Write your answer on the lines.

4. How can an employee learn about a company's corporate culture?

   _____

   _____

Match the term on the left to the correct definition on the right.

5. conduct   A. building relationships with other people to help your career

6. hazard   B. a more experienced employee who helps train a new worker

7. mentor   C. your behavior

8. networking   D. the time you are scheduled to work

9. shift   E. the steps you follow in order to do something

10. procedure   F. danger

Being Professional

GOALS

▶ LEARN what it means to be professional

▶ THINK ABOUT which behaviors are appropriate at work

▶ LEARN about online social networking and work

TERMS

self-discipline the ability to make yourself do things that need to be done

direct reports employees who work for a supervisor

What does it mean to be professional? It means acting polite and respectful. It also means acting in a businesslike way. This includes a wide range of skills and actions:

▶ Arrive on time for work.
▶ Follow company policies.
▶ Dress appropriately.
▶ Use good personal hygiene (brush your teeth, shower, etc.).

Being professional also means that you take responsibility for your work. You should focus on the tasks you are given. Check in with your supervisor often. Be honest and polite when you speak to   about your work.

Outside of the Workplace

At times, your conduct may be judged even when you are not at work. Suppose you go to lunch with some of your co-workers. Even though you are not at work, these co-workers may judge your behavior. If you eat too quickly, make noise when chewing, or talk with your mouth full, they may think you are rude. By acting like a professional, you can make a good impression.

Sometimes, you need to act like a professional even when you're not with your co-workers. Suppose you go to the mall with a friend. The two of you get into an argument. What if someone you work with is also at the mall? If your boss sees you arguing, it might affect what she thinks of you. You never know who you might see—or who might see you.

Like it or not, when you are in public, you will be judged by others. People form opinions about you and your work habits from your conduct. So be alert and behave like a professional.

Professional Behaviors

This scene shows workers in a store. Study each part of the scene and read the labels. Circle the workers who are behaving like professionals. Draw an *X* over the workers who are not acting like professionals.

Talking with a co-worker about a work task

Texting during work hours

Wearing clothes you would wear to a nightclub

Arriving late to work

Helping a customer at the cash register

Folding clothes

JOB TEAM

Work is *Every* Day

Good employees act like professionals. They also have self-discipline. **Self-discipline** means you have the willpower to do the things that need to be done or that others expect of you.

Keep in mind that when you take a job, you are making a promise to do your best work. You may have days when you feel like staying home from work. You might be tired or upset. But you have to overcome these feelings and go to work anyway. Showing up is key to keeping and succeeding in your job.

Professional Behavior

Professional behavior is not just how you do your job. Being professional also includes the way you act while you are at work. Avoid gossip. Don't talk about other employees. Keep your personal opinions to yourself. Don't talk about topics that could offend a co-worker, such as politics or religion.

In general, you should avoid discussions that are not related to work. They take your focus away from your job. They can also lead to hard feelings and, at times, trouble.

You may have little in common with some of your co-workers. You may not like some of them. You don't have to be best friends with your co-workers. But you do need to work well together.

This is also true of supervisors. They must be professional when working with their **direct reports.** Direct reports are the employees who work for or report to a supervisor.

Co-workers should act like professionals, too. You should always be treated with respect. If someone treats you badly, report it to your supervisor. You may also report it to human resources.

At the same time, remember that everyone has a bad day once in a while. If a co-worker gets upset with you one day, give him a chance to apologize. Do not let someone else's behavior affect your work.

Activity

Personal or Professional?

Read the statements below. Then decide if the conversation is appropriate for work. Is the conversation personal or professional? Circle your answer.

1. Dr. Roberts likes the way that Janie makes notes on his patients' charts. He asks her, "Janie, would you please show the other nurses how you've made these notes?"
   PERSONAL   PROFESSIONAL

2. Marina and Kirk are in the staff break room. Marina asks Kirk what he did over the weekend. Kirk says, "I got so drunk on Saturday night!"
   PERSONAL   PROFESSIONAL

3. A group of workers is chatting while waiting for a meeting to start. An employee named Chris enters the room and asks the group, "Did you guys see the president's speech last night? I love this president!"
   PERSONAL   PROFESSIONAL

Social Networking

Online social networking sites have become popular. If you're like many workers, you use one or more of these sites. Sites such as Facebook and Twitter can be great for keeping in touch with others.

You should avoid posting information about your company or co-workers on these sites. Employers often keep track of workers' use of these sites. They take what they read seriously.

You should also be careful when posting pictures of yourself. This is especially true when posting from the computers at work. You should not post pictures or updates to your personal site while you are at work.

Don't post about work-related problems. Suppose you get angry with someone at work. You might be tempted to post a negative comment. This is a bad idea. These posts can be seen by more people than you might think. Don't risk losing your job by posting about your job or co-workers.

Working Effectively

GOALS

▶ LEARN about group dynamics

▶ COMPLETE group and individual activities

▶ COMPARE leadership styles

TERMS

group dynamic how people act in a group

Groups at work often include employees of different cultures and backgrounds. Everyone must work together.

We all belong to different groups. Our groups could be

▶ family
▶ friends
▶ a class
▶ a sports team

Each of these groups has a **group dynamic.** A group dynamic is how people act in a group and how the group members interact with each other. Every group will have both leaders and followers. This is true in most workplaces. Supervisors often act as leaders, while employees act as followers.

At work, it's OK to be a follower. You will need to figure out how to fit in with the rest of your group at work. It's the leader's job to see that group members work well together. It's also the leader's job to see that each person has a chance to add something to the group.

As a follower, it is your job to speak up and take part in the group's tasks. This is the best way for your boss to see the quality of your work. Every worker needs to know how to work well in a group.

Though employees often act as followers, it's OK to sometimes show you can be a leader. Don't be afraid to speak up and offer appropriate suggestions. Don't be too bossy. This can help show that you might make a good supervisor someday.

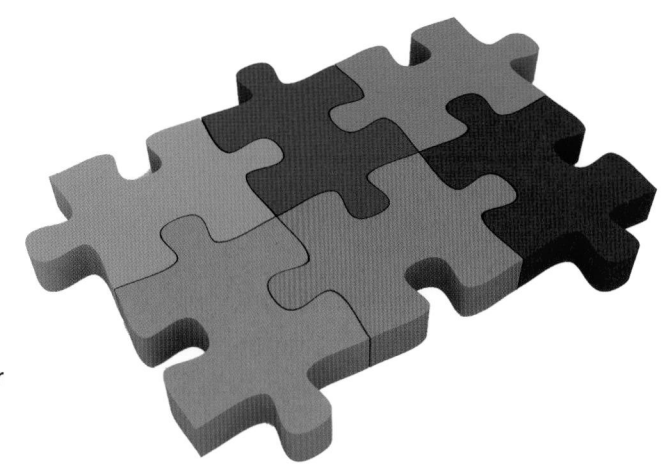

Activity

The Group Dynamic

Your teacher will divide your class into groups. Each group will receive a jigsaw puzzle to complete. As your group puts together the puzzle, think about how you are working as a group. When your group has completed the puzzle, answer the questions below. These questions will help you look at your group's dynamic. Then use your answers to discuss this activity as a class.

How Well Did You Do?

1. How well did you work with your group? Did you act as a leader or as a follower?

2. Did you do your best to help solve the puzzle? Or did you sit back and allow others to do the work?

3. Did you take over the project and not let the others share the work?

4. How did you feel about working in a group? Did your group work together successfully?

Working on Your Own

Even when you work as part of a team, you may still have tasks to do on your own. You may be responsible for your own part of a larger project. In this way, you are working independently but also as part of a team.

Working alone has some advantages. It can make you feel free. But it can cause problems. To work well on your own, you need self-discipline. You won't have other team members to encourage you and keep you focused on your work.

Use this checklist to help you stay on track when working alone:

- ❏ **List big steps:** Before you start, make a list of the big steps you need to take.

- ❏ **Plan your time:** Make your best guess as to how long you will need to complete each step.

- ❏ **List small steps:** Break down each big step into a list of smaller steps.

- ❏ **Check off steps:** As you finish a small or big step, check it off. Keep track of your progress!

- ❏ **Check in with co-workers:** Ask them what they think. This will help you know if you are doing the job right. It may also give you ideas to improve your work.

- ❏ **Check in with your supervisor:** Let her know that you are on track. It will also give her a chance to share any new information.

- ❏ **Check your work:** Take time to check your work before you say it's finished. This shows that you take your job seriously.

Mark makes the pizzas by himself, but he needs Tommy to make the crust. Brea is the cashier. She needs Mark to check that the orders are correct and on time.

Suppose you work in a shoe store. You have to organize the back storeroom. What if you don't understand some parts of the task? In a case like this, it's important to ask for help. Talk to your boss so you can be sure you understand your assignment. Talk to him before you begin and when you have questions. When you work alone, you are responsible for your own work. It is up to you to do a good job.

What if you are assigned to do a part of a large group project? Check in with other group members. You need to know you are all working toward the same goal.

Think about the job of organizing the back storeroom of the shoe store. What if it was assigned to four workers? You would need to know how the other workers were organizing their parts. Are shoes grouped by size? Color? The shoe maker? You would all want to use the same system. Working well with other group members shows respect. It also helps you get the job done well.

Activity

Work on Your Own

Follow the instructions below to make an origami star. Work on your own. You'll have five minutes to complete your star. When your project is complete, answer the questions below. These will help you judge how well you work on your own. (Teacher: cut a standard sheet of paper lengthwise into eight equal strips.)

1. Begin with a strip of paper. Tie a knot in the end of your paper.

2. Pull gently until it's tight. Flatten knot.

3. Next fold the short end of the paper strip down (toward the center of the knot). Tuck it into the knot. If it's too long to tuck in, fold or cut it to fit.

4. Wrap the other end of the strip around the knot, over and over. Keep wrapping until you get to the end of the strip.

5. Now tuck the end of the strip into the knot.

6. To make the star puff out, gently press on each of its edges.

How Well Did You Do?

1. How would you judge your work on this task?

2. Were you able to stay on task for the entire time? Did you find yourself losing focus?

3. Did you complete the task on time?

4. Did you ask for help if you needed it?

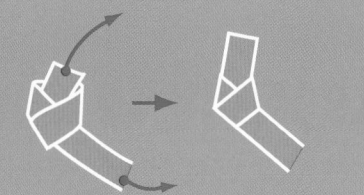
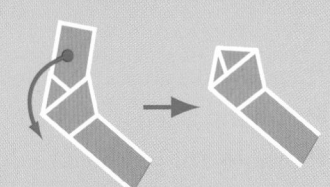
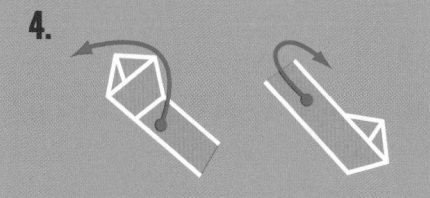
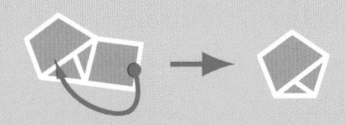
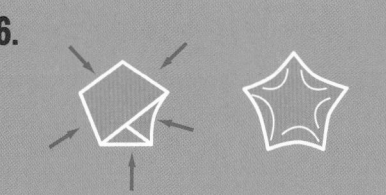

JOB & LIFE SKILLS

Self-Discipline

The self-discipline you need at work is a lot like what you need in everyday life. When you live alone, you clean your own home and cook your own meals. If you don't do it, no one will. You should approach your job in the same way. Don't expect your co-workers to do your tasks for you. Take ownership of what you're assigned. Expect to do your best work every day.

Leadership and Teamwork

Learning to Lead

Good leaders find ways to help others succeed. A good supervisor leads a team by

▶ showing a clear purpose
▶ giving a sense of direction
▶ motivating others to do their best

A supervisor's leadership style affects how well his department runs. This style also controls how problems are solved. There are many types of leadership styles. This table describes four of the most common styles. Read and discuss the examples.

A good boss must be a good leader. But what makes a good leader, and how can you develop such skills? One way is to study the behavior of strong leaders. The following activities give you the chance to study both good and poor leadership styles. This will help when you are put in the role of leader.

TYPES OF LEADERS

Leadership Style	Style Description	What This Leader May Say
By the book	In this style, all tasks must be done the way the manuals say. If the manual doesn't cover it, the leader checks with his boss.	"The company policy states that…" "I'm not sure if that is allowed. I will check and get back to you." "Work hours are from 8 to 5."
Hands-off	This type of leader gives workers great freedom in their daily duties. They must set goals, make decisions, and solve problems on their own.	"Whatever you think will work best." "You two take care of the problem."
My way or the highway	This leader tells her employees what she wants done and how she wants it done. She doesn't ask her workers for ideas. She doesn't explain her orders.	"Because I said so!" "Don't ask questions." "Just do it." "I didn't ask for your opinion."
Asks for input	In this style, the leader includes his workers when making decisions. However, he has final say on each decision.	"What do you think?" "I'd like to hear from everyone before I make a decision."

Role Play: Leadership Styles

Joseph works for a company that requires all employees to wear a uniform. He does not always come to work in a complete uniform. Some days Joseph wears jeans instead of the tan pants that are part of the uniform. On other days, he is not wearing a nametag. Joseph's boss and co-workers are aware of the problem.

Some co-workers believe Joseph's dress code problems are because of poor planning. Others believe he is ignoring the rules on purpose. If you were Joseph's boss, how would you handle the situation? To find out, role-play a discussion with Joseph and each of the following supervisors:

- "by-the-book" boss

- "hands-off" boss

- "my-way-or-the-highway" boss

- boss who asks for input

Place two chairs in the middle of the room facing each other. Have students take turns playing the roles of Joseph and his bosses. Role-play a discussion with Joseph about the dress code. Be sure students follow each leader's style.

Group Discussion

1. Which leadership style worked the best?

2. What could each leader have done differently?

3. How would the "perfect" leader handle this situation?

Follow up activity: Think about leaders you have now or have had in the past. As a group, discuss the characteristics of good leaders and poor leaders. Make lists of good qualities and poor qualities. If you have not had a boss, list qualities from the role play.

Resolving Conflicts

GOALS

▶ LEARN the steps to resolve conflict at work

▶ ROLE PLAY being a supervisor

▶ LEARN about working styles

TERMS

compromise a way to reach an agreement in which each person or group gives up something

generation a group of people born and living during the same time

retire to end a job or career

Workplaces can be busy and stressful. They bring many people together, often under stress or pressure. So it is no surprise that people often have conflicts at work. Conflicts can be a difference of opinion, a major disagreement, or a fight for power.

Many things can lead to conflict in the workplace. These might include:

▶ simple misunderstandings
▶ poor communication
▶ different working styles
▶ gossip

Conflict is a natural result of working with others. Most people will experience a conflict with a co-worker. Although conflict at work is common, you should always deal with it. Ignoring a conflict will not make it go away. In fact, it is more likely to grow into a larger problem.

You should learn to spot conflicts early. Then you can take steps to fix things quickly. Often, people fix or resolve conflicts by coming to a compromise. A **compromise** is a way to reach an agreement in which each person or group gives up something. It is rare when one person is completely right and another is completely wrong. So each one giving a little makes sense. Here is a list of steps you can use to resolve conflicts.

Steps to Resolve a Conflict

1. **Try** to find the exact cause of the conflict.

2. **Ask** each person to clearly tell his side of the conflict.

3. **Encourage** each person to consider the other person's view.

4. **Ask** each person to describe how she would like the problem solved. Compare their solutions.

5. **Brainstorm** possible ideas that could lead to a compromise.

6. **Choose** the solution that works best for all, especially for your company.

Conflict Resolution

Read about three conflicts at work. Look at each conflict from both sides. Re-read the steps on page 46. Use them to suggest possible ways to compromise. Discuss your suggestions as a class.

Conflict 1: Sabeen and Tanya work at desks that are next to each other. Sabeen is very friendly and outgoing. Tanya is quieter and keeps to herself. Sabeen makes many personal calls from her desk. This annoys Tanya, who finds the calls distracting. She reports Sabeen for breaking the rules. Only some of her complaints are true. Tanya is trying to get Sabeen fired.

Conflict 2: James has been with a plumbing company for more than 30 years. He does not have a plumber's license, but he has had many years of experience. Mick just started working at the company. He has his plumber's license. James is upset because others at the company see Mick as the expert on plumbing. But Mick has only been with the company for a few months. James is jealous of Mick and criticizes every idea that he has. Mick feels that James does not respect him, so he does not treat James with respect.

Conflict 3: Carlos and Suzanne are two computer techs in the same hospital. They both hope to be named head of the technology department. Each complains about the other's work all the time. Both are good at their jobs, and the problems they complain about are small. Their fighting has gotten so bad, the other techs have complained to the human resources staff. If Carlos and Suzanne keep complaining, neither will be named head of the department.

The Role of the Supervisor

Have you ever been in an argument in which both sides refused to give in? As you tried harder to work things out, did it get worse? When conflicts like this happen at work, you may have to turn to your supervisor to work them out.

Often, workers will choose to resolve conflicts on their own. When you involve a supervisor, it makes the conflict more formal. Your supervisor may be required to file a report. She may also have to discipline or punish you or your co-worker.

If you decide to talk to your supervisor, give your point of view objectively. Tell him the facts. Focus on what happened, not on your feelings.

Write down what your co-worker has done or said to offend you. Give your supervisor the list. Do not insult your co-worker.

At times, you may have a conflict with your supervisor. If you do, try to work it out with her. If you can't, you may need to talk to someone with more authority (power) than your supervisor. In some workplaces, this may be a person in human resources. In others, it may be your supervisor's boss.

Activity

Role Play: Be the Supervisor

Two servers in a restaurant are having a conflict. It is up to the manager to help them work it out.

Work with two classmates. Read about the conflict below. Then act out the meeting. Two of you will be the employees and one will be the manager. Use what you've learned from the lesson. Write about how you resolved the conflict.

- Employee A is hard-working and experienced. She often helps new servers as they learn about their jobs.

- Employee B is a new server. He has begun to take advantage of A's helpfulness. Employee B does not work very hard. He counts on A to do some of his work.

- Employee A has finally had enough. She demands a share of B's tips. B argues that this is unfair.

- The restaurant manager must resolve the conflict between A and B. She should guide them to work out their problems.

Resolution:

_____

_____

_____

_____

_____

_____

_____

Working With All Generations

A **generation** is a group of people born and living during the same time. This timeline shows four generations alive today and what they are called.

Born between	1922–1945	1946–1964	1965–1980	1981–2000
Nicknames	Veterans, Traditionalists	Baby Boomers	Generation X Gen X	Generation Y Millennials, Echo Boomers

1900   1910   1920   1930   1940   1950   1960   1970   1980   1990   2000

When people **retire,** they stop working at jobs or careers. Many older workers are retiring later. This means there are more older workers in jobs. It also means that four generations are now working together for the first time.

The generation you belong to can affect how you look at things. It affects your attitudes and the way you perform at work. One generation often finds it hard to understand the others.

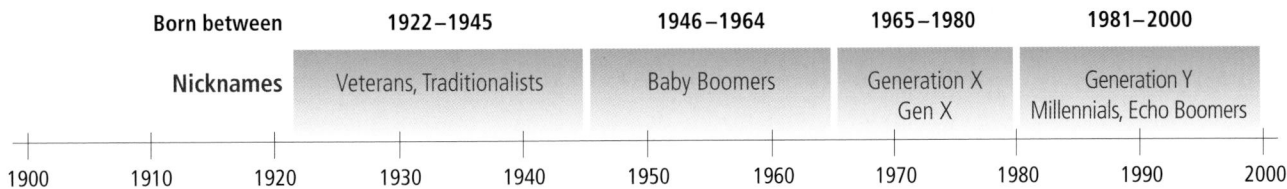

You'll want to work out or even avoid conflicts at work. This will be easier if you understand how the generations differ from each other.

The table below explains the working styles of people of different generations.

WORKING STYLES OF THE GENERATIONS

	Veterans (born 1922-1945)	Baby Boomers (born 1946-1964)	Generation X (born 1965-1980)	Generation Y (born 1981-2000)
Main Values	Respect for authority; discipline	Hopeful; involved	Questioning others; fun-loving; informal	Realistic; confident; fun-loving; social
Family Style	Traditional, two-parent household	Changing; some single-parent households	Two-income households; children often home alone	Multiple marriages; combined families
Communication Style	One-on-one; formal letters	Landline phones; in-person meetings	Cell phones; e-mail; person-to-person	Smart phones; mobile devices
Work Values	Hard working; work comes before fun	Workaholics; personal success; question authority	Rely on self; prefer structure and direction	Multi-tasking; goal-focused
Leadership Style	Direct; firm	Treat people like equals	Everyone's equal; challenge others; ask why	Work as a team; take risks
What Motivates Them	Respect their experience	Tell them they are valued and needed	Have them do it their own way	Tell them they will work with other bright, creative people

Customer Service

GOALS

▶ LEARN strategies for good customer service

▶ ROLE PLAY ways to work with unhappy customers

▶ PRACTICE good customer service skills

TERMS

customer a person or a group who buys goods or uses services from a business

customer service the help that a company gives to the people who buy its products or use its services

support staff workers who help other employees do their work

Customer service starts with the customer. A **customer** can be a person or a group who buys goods or uses services from a business. A customer is someone who buys things in a store. It could also be a patient in a doctor's office. It could be a factory that buys the parts that a company makes.

Customer service is the help that a business gives to the people who buy its products or services. In a way, almost every job involves some customer service skills.

Think about the jobs you have had. Who were your customers? How did you work with them in these jobs? If you aren't sure who your customers were, look at the table. It lists some jobs and some of the customers for each one.

Job	Who are the customers?
Farmer	Grocery stores, restaurants, families
Real estate agent	Home buyers and sellers
Painter	Construction companies, homeowners
RN (registered nurse)	Patients in a doctor's office or hospital
Police officer	Citizens of a local area

Taking Care of Co-Workers

The Information Technology (IT) department at this company is always busy.

Their customers are also their co-workers.

They provide tech support and fix computers.

Internal Customers

It's obvious that people standing at a checkout counter are customers. But some people help customers who are also their co-workers. People who have these jobs are called support staff. A **support staff** includes the workers who support the work of the other employees. They include receptionists, secretaries, assistants, and tech workers.

There are support staff workers in every field. Often, support staff work with both internal and external customers. A doctor's assistant supports the doctor. This is his internal support job. He also supports the doctor's patients. This is his external support job. It is important that support staff satisfy both types of customers.

Some support workers serve many internal customers. Kara is the assistant to a company CEO. Her main duties are to assist the CEO. But she works with other staff members, too. Kara trains new staff on how to file reports. She also makes travel plans for other staff. Kara helps many people, but she never forgets her main work for the CEO.

JOB TALK

PROFESSIONAL COMMUNICATION

Good customer service is needed in many jobs. Use the following tips to give good customer service in your job.

Be Professional

All businesses depend on their customers. You should treat them in a professional way at all times. Remain calm. Treat your customers with respect. This shows customers that you are serious about their business.

Speak Clearly

Speaking clearly is a key part of customer service. When customers have a problem, they want someone to listen and then respond clearly. Customers can grow frustrated when workers speak too softly or mumble. This makes it hard to solve the customer's problem.

Listen Actively

Active listening is a great skill in customer service. Listen closely while the customer is speaking. Don't interrupt. Pay attention to the customer. Don't get distracted. Focus on what the customer is saying. Ask questions to make sure you understand.

Restate

When you restate or paraphrase something, you say it in your own words. Restating what customers say helps you to be sure you heard them correctly. It also shows that you understand their needs. This will help you solve problems more effectively.

Dissatisfied Customers

At times, both internal and external customers may not be satisfied. Customers may feel they did not get proper service. They may be unhappy with a product they bought. It is the job of customer service to make the situation right.

If you work with customers, at some point you will have to work with an unhappy one. The key is to listen to his complaint and try to correct the problem. Always be polite and respectful. If you deal with the problem well, you may end up with a happy customer.

Making Things Right

Joel is a customer service representative for a restaurant called Fresh Eats. One day, he receives a call from Hector Agosto. Hector's family had a bad experience the last time they visited Fresh Eats. Read the conversation to see how Joel fixes the problem.

Joel: Hello, thanks for calling Fresh Eats. How may I help you?

Hector: My name is Hector Agosto. My family and I were at Fresh Eats last night. It was the worst meal I've ever had.

Joel: I'm so sorry, Mr. Agosto. Tell me what happened.

(By asking what happened, Joel shows that he cares about what happened to Hector and his family.)

Hector: Well, the service was lousy. We waited 10 minutes before anyone came to take our order. It was another 45 minutes before our food arrived. And when you have kids, it's really hard for them to wait that long. They shouldn't have to wait that long.

Joel: No, sir, they shouldn't.

(Joel lets Hector explain what happened. This shows Hector that Joel is interested in what he has to say. By agreeing with Hector, Joel is helping to keep him calm.)

Hector: When the food did arrive, two of our orders were wrong. We just ate what we were served because we couldn't wait any longer to eat.

Joel: Mr. Agosto, I'm really sorry this happened. At Fresh Eats, our goal is for each family to be served quickly and treated with respect. We expect every order to be correct. Please allow me to refund the cost of your meal. I would also like to give you a $25 gift card for your next meal at Fresh Eats.

(By apologizing, Joel tries to lessen Hector's anger. Joel also suggests a solution to make up for Hector's bad experience. He hopes Hector and his family will try Fresh Eats again. He does not want to lose a customer.)

I'm also going to discuss this problem with our servers. I'll find out why you had such a long wait. We will make sure it does not happen again.

(This is to convince Hector that if his family does return to the restaurant, the service will be better.)

Hector: Well, I appreciate that. I'll stop by tonight for the refund and to pick up the gift card.

Joel: Great! I'll let the hostess know to expect you. Thank you, sir, for letting me know about your experience.

(Thanking Hector for his call tells him that his business and input are valued.)

Role Play: The Unhappy Customer

For this activity, you will work with a partner. Use what you've learned about working with unhappy customers to act out this scene. One person plays the role of the customer, while the other is the server.

A customer goes to a restaurant on Friday at 2:15 p.m. for a late lunch. He thinks he has ordered from the lunch menu and should pay lunchtime prices. However, on Fridays the restaurant stops their lunchtime prices at 2 p.m. After 2 p.m., the prices go up and the serving size does also.

When the check comes, the customer sees he was charged a full dinner price. He complains that he was overcharged.

Write what you and your partner will say. Act out the conversation.

Do your best to calm the customer and solve the problem.

Remember these tips:

- Listen actively
- Ask questions
- Apologize
- Offer a solution

Customer:	Excuse me. I think my bill is wrong. I was overcharged.
Server:	It is after 2:00, sir. I had to charge you the dinner price.

Customer: _____

_____

Server: _____

_____

Customer: _____

_____

Server: _____

_____

Customer: _____

_____

Server: _____

_____

Role Play: The Needy Patient

For this activity, you will work with a partner. The scene takes place in a nursing home. One of you will play a busy Licensed Practical Nurse (LPN). The other will play a patient. The patient spends a great deal of time talking to the LPN. This prevents the LPN from completing his/her work duties. The LPN must tell the patient that he/she needs to go see other patients.

Remember to be kind when dealing with the patient. Patients are often worried, scared, upset, or in pain. This can make them difficult to deal with, so you should be kind and patient.

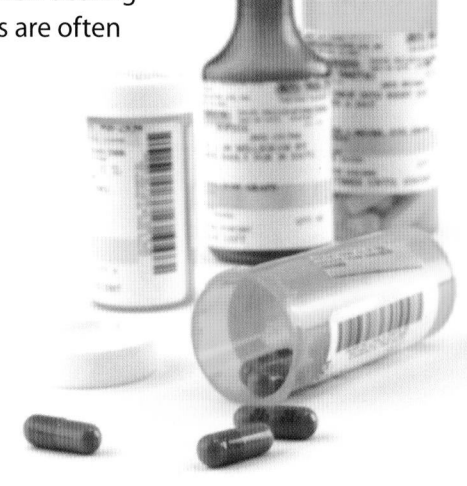

Role Play: Taking an Order

In this scene, one person plays the role of a park manager. The other acts as the owner of a gardening business. The manager orders some gardening work for the park. The gardener asks questions and writes down all the information.

For example, the park manager may ask for flower beds around the parking lot. The gardener may then ask what kind of flowers the park needs and how many. Each should restate what the other says to be sure they understand.

Making Math Easier

In your workplace, you may need to do tasks such as placing orders or figuring costs. These jobs require a lot of math. There are computer programs to make these jobs easier.

You may have already worked with software programs that can organize data quickly. Some programs can also perform math calculations much faster than a person could.

Some companies use software programs to create spreadsheets. These spreadsheets can track inventory (stock), bills, and payments. It is important to be familiar with computers. Almost all jobs today require some computer skills. If you take basic computer classes, you'll increase your chance of landing a job or getting a promotion.

Even if you have worked with computers, you may still need to learn the special programs your company uses. Taking classes in basic computer programs will help you understand how they work. This will also help you get up to speed quickly at a new job.

Activity

Calculate Percentages

Everyone uses basic math skills—whether they are workers or customers. You may need to calculate a discount on an item you are buying or the tip at a restaurant. Many of these calculations use percentages.

A percentage is a part of a larger whole. The whole is 100 percent. The part is expresses in hundredths. For example, 10 percent is 10x out of 100 or 10 hundredths.

You can calculate percentages by multiplying. For example, to find out what 20 percent of $15.00 is, multiply .20 (20 hundredths) by 15. (.20 × 15 = 3)

Practice calculating percentages. You can use a calculator.

Nicolai had his hair cut for $20. He wants to give the stylist a 15% tip. How much should he give her?

_____

Maria wants to buy a new skirt. Next week the skirt will be 20% off. If the skirt costs $35, how much will she save if she buys it next week?

_____

Ken sells used cars. His customer has only $4,000 to spend. The car he is looking at costs $3,600. The tax on the car is 8%. How much will the car cost with tax?

_____

Managing Stress

GOALS

► LEARN about stress and its causes

► PLAN ways to reduce stress

► LEARN to spot stress at work and handle it

TERMS

stress mental pressure or worry

stressors events that cause stress

Carmen's day was off to a bad start. She had an argument with her daughter, who refused to get dressed for school. When she finally dropped off the unhappy girl, Carmen noticed she had a flat tire. A friend helped her change the tire, but this made Carmen late to work. As she hurried inside, her boss asked, "Why didn't you call?" Carmen nearly cried. What a bad way to start the day!

Like many people, Carmen was reacting to stress. **Stress** is something that causes strong feelings of worry. Events that cause stress are **stressors.** In this case, Carmen had many stressors, all in the same morning. She became so upset that she couldn't focus on her job. Problems outside of work were what caused Carmen to become stressed.

Many parts of a person's life can cause stress. People may feel stressed over money or family issues. Even good changes, such as getting married or having a baby, can cause stress.

It is important to keep stressors out of your work so you can focus on your job. Carmen won't have to deal with her daughter's bad attitude or the flat tire while she's at work. The issues may still be there when she goes home. But thinking about stress while at work will only make things worse.

Activity

What Are Your Stressors?

Think about your daily life and routines. What causes you stress? As you think of your stressors, consider how you react to them. For example, some people become aggressive or angry. Others cry or walk away. Stressors cause some to shut down completely. By understanding how you respond to stress, you can work to manage it.

Write down your stressors and how you react to them. Then work with your teacher to identify some safe ways to calm down when stressed. Write an action plan. Your plan should list ways of coping with stress—both in daily life and on the job.

Handling Stress

Everyone feels stress at times. You can't always control when you might begin to feel stress. But you can control how this stress affects you. At times you may want to just walk away from stress. But you can't walk away from your job responsibilities just because of stress.

It's important to develop ways to deal with your stress. You need to be able to work through it and meet your responsibilities. The scenes below show five examples of people dealing with stress. The text describes poor and better ways of dealing with it. Which one of these good stress relievers do you think will work the best for you?

Avoid acting out toward others. Instead, get rid of stress by some other type of physical activity. Running or lifting weights can both help to ease stress.

Don't withdraw or become too emotional. Instead, try to relax and focus on the main parts of the problem. This might include praying or meditating. You might also go for a hike, take a long bath, or listen to music.

Resist abusing cigarettes or alcohol to cope with stress. Instead, try speaking to someone about the cause of your stress. This could be a friend, family member, mentor, or pastor.

At times, stress may cause you to exaggerate a problem. Don't make the problem bigger than it is. Take a step back, and look at the problem objectively. If possible, try to sleep on the problem. With a bit of time, it may seem easier to deal with.

Sometimes you may be tempted to take your stress out on others. Instead of creating conflict, try to be honest about your feelings. Instead of arguing, try to discuss the real causes of your stress. Friends and family will be more supportive if you are honest.

Stress on the Job

Sometimes your job can cause you stress. Feeling overworked or   can cause stress. Conflict with a supervisor or co-worker can, too.

You should look for ways to ease the stress you feel at work. You should also let people know that you are feeling stressed. You might tell your supervisor or someone in the human resources office. Talking to someone about feeling stressed can help you to feel better.

JOB & LIFE SKILLS

Stress Relief

What can you do if you are at work and you feel stressed? You may be too busy to talk to someone. You may not be able to take a break.

Here is a simple breathing exercise you can do anytime, anywhere. Studies show that deep breathing can relax you and improve your health. This exercise can slow your heart rate and lower your blood pressure. That might be just what you need to get through a stressful day.

Breathe to Relieve Stress

1. Sit in a comfortable position. Close your eyes.

2. Clear your mind of work or other stressful thoughts. If it helps, imagine yourself in a relaxing place.

3. Put one hand on your stomach. Breathe in through your nose while you count to five. Feel the air fill your stomach while you breathe in.

4. Breathe out slowly through your mouth while you count to eight.

5. Repeat three or four times.

FINDING SOLUTIONS

Read about ways these workers can handle stress at work.

Airline: Ticket Agent

This airline worker must deal with a long line of unhappy customers. To ease her stress, she should alert her co-workers and supervisor. She should ask for help so that the customers' needs can be met quickly.

Airline: Flight Attendant

This flight attendant is often left behind by her co-workers after a break. They walk ahead as a group, and she can't catch up to them. They tell her when they are planning to leave the break room. But she is not usually ready when they are. She should see that her behavior is the problem. She needs to be on time in the future.

Restaurant: Cook

These cooks have been asked by their supervisor to work late. It has been a busy day, and they are angry about staying late. Rather than lashing out, they should take a break to calm down. Then they can return to their work without stress.

Restaurant: Chef

The restaurant's servers have not told this chef what he needs to know so he can cook the orders correctly. Rather than yelling at the servers, the chef should explain the problem calmly and clearly. He needs to tell the servers how this problem affects him and their orders. This may convince them to change their behavior.

Carpentry: New Worker

This carpenter is stressed because she has not been trained how to run a machine. To ease her stress, she should ask her supervisor for the proper training. Using a machine in the wrong way is not safe. This will only cause more stress.

Carpentry: Co-workers

These carpenters disagree about how to do a job. To relieve their stress, they should seek out their supervisor. He can help them resolve the issue quickly and prevent the situation from getting worse.

Check off the goals you achieved in Chapter 2.

In Lesson 1, you . . .

☐ Learned what it means to be professional

☐ Thought about which behaviors are appropriate at work

☐ Learned about online social networking and work

In Lesson 2, you . . .

☐ Learned about group dynamics

☐ Completed group and individual activities

☐ Compared leadership styles

In Lesson 3, you . . .

☐ Learned the steps to resolve conflict at work

☐ Role-played being a supervisor

☐ Learned about working styles

In Lesson 4, you . . .

☐ Learned strategies for good customer service

☐ Role-played ways to work with unhappy customers

☐ Practiced good customer service skills

In Lesson 5, you . . .

☐ Learned about stress and its causes

☐ Planned ways to reduce stress

☐ Learned how to spot stress at work and handle it

What do you want to know more about?

List the things that you want to learn more about. Talk to your teacher or look them up online.

Choose the best answer.

1. Which is the best way to relieve workplace stress?

   A. abusing cigarettes or alcohol

   B. taking a deep breath and finding help

   C. walking away from your workplace

   D. physically acting out toward your co-workers

True or false? If the statement is true, write *T*. If the statement is false, write *F*. Then change the false statement to make it true.

2. Working in a group requires more self-discipline than working independently.

   _____

3. Almost every job requires employees to use some type of customer service skills.

   _____

Write your answer on the lines.

4. Why is it important to show professionalism outside of the workplace?

   _____

   _____

Match the term on the left to the correct definition on the right.

5. conflict

6. compromise

7. group dynamic

8. hygiene

9. professional

10. customer service

A. a way to reach an agreement in which each person gives up something

B. polite, respectful, and businesslike

C. a disagreement or argument

D. the help that a company gives to people who buy its products

E. things you do to be clean and healthy

F. how people act in a group

Self-Esteem on the Job

GOALS

▶ LEARN how self-esteem can affect your work

▶ WRITE about the successes that build your self-esteem

▶ PLAN to build your self-esteem at work

TERMS

self-esteem a feeling of pride and confidence in yourself

Carla Marquez could not stop smiling as she rode the bus home from work. Carla works as an assistant to a veterinarian. That morning, a man brought his dog into the vet's office. Carla was the first to see the dog. She knew right away the dog was very sick. She told the vet. He rushed the dog into surgery and saved its life.

After the operation, the vet praised Carla. If she had not told him about the dog so quickly, the dog would have died. Hearing the vet praise her work made Carla feel good. It lifted her self-esteem. **Self-esteem** is a feeling of pride and confidence in yourself.

Like Carla, many people build their self-esteem by accomplishing things. You might complete an important task at work or reach a personal goal. These accomplishments make you feel good about yourself. Having good self-esteem can be useful in all parts of life. It gives you energy and makes you want to succeed.

Activity

Be Your Own Cheerleader

You build self-esteem when you recognize and take pride in your own successes. Think back. What are some of your proudest moments? It might have been when you graduated from high school. It might have been when you helped someone learn a new skill. Try to recall both personal and professional accomplishments. Then list or draw them on a sheet of paper.

You Are Important

You may know workers who complain about their jobs. They may not trust the companies they work for. They may think that their employers don't respect them.

Most employers do value their workers. They think their workers are important. Successful businesses spend time and money to train their workers. They want their workers to succeed. Employers work hard to keep good workers. They don't want to drive them away.

Amy is the manager of a local bank. Amy values her workers. She knows their work helps her bank succeed. She feels all the employees are in it together.

Amy admits that a few managers may be out for themselves. They are more interested in their own success than in what's good for the bank. But she thinks most of them appreciate their workers.

Amy tells her staff, "I don't want to criticize you. I want to cheer you on. I want to praise you for what you do well. And I want to work with you to improve the areas that are hard for you. I hope you will listen to what I say. I want to help you succeed!"

Several of Amy's employees have been promoted to better jobs in the company. Instead of being upset at losing them, Amy feels proud and wishes them well. She thinks having workers who do well is one of the best parts of her job.

Amy began as a teller and is now a vice-president. Her bosses could see her positive attitude and how it helped the bank every day. This helped make her a success.

Good employers show they appreciate the work you do. They may do this by giving awards or simply by saying "thank you."

Work Increases Self-Esteem

Reyna is a phlebotomist. She uses needles to take blood samples from patients. Reyna is proud of her job skills. They add to her sense of self-esteem.

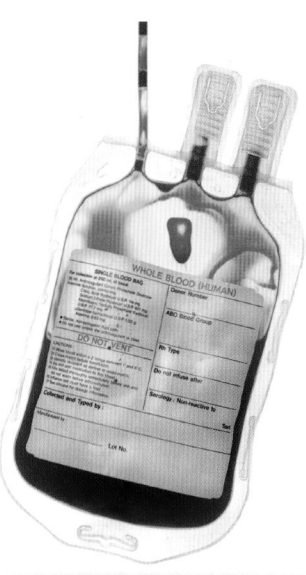

Reyna helps people deal with their fear of needles and blood.

Reyna can get a job in many places, such as hospitals, labs, doctors' offices, blood banks, and clinics.

She has tricks to distract children so the needle won't hurt.

Her job requires training, certification, and experience. These make her feel confident in her work skills.

She helps sick people get better.

Building Self-Esteem

Many workers struggle with self-esteem at work. This is especially true of new workers. There are many ways to build your self-esteem at work. These strategies can help you to feel confident in your job.

- ▶ **Behave confidently.** When you believe in yourself, others will take notice. When you act confident, you will feel confident.
- ▶ **Speak strongly and clearly.** Others will listen more carefully to you.
- ▶ **Walk with confidence.** Stand up straight. It is easier to believe in someone who walks confidently.
- ▶ **Connect with positive people.** They are more likely to give you encouragement. This will help build your self-esteem. At the same time, you should encourage others.
- ▶ **Set daily work goals.** Make a checklist of the goals you set for yourself. Then check off each goal as you reach it.
- ▶ **Take pride in your accomplishments.** You should feel proud when you accomplish something. Every time you reach a goal, you will build self-esteem.

Acting with confidence is the first step toward being confident!

JOB & LIFE SKILLS

Keep Your Focus

Personal problems can affect how well you do your job. They can also lower your self-esteem.

Try to keep personal problems separate from work. For instance, you may be upset about problems at home. Or perhaps you and a friend had a fight. You may feel sad or worried. However, it's important that you don't let these feelings affect your work.

Remember that your employer is depending on you to do your job well. Even though it may be hard, try not to let things that lower your self-esteem affect your work. If you continue to do your job well, your self-esteem should remain high. Feeling good about your work may even help you get through difficult times in your personal life.

GOALS

▶ LEARN how feedback is helpful at work

▶ READ about strategies for using feedback to improve your work

▶ PRACTICE giving feedback

TERMS

feedback helpful information that is given to show what can be done to improve something

Feedback

Feedback is helpful information that is given to show how you can improve something.

It is a word that can scare many workers. Some think that feedback is all negative. But it isn't meant to be. Feedback shows you ways in which you can improve. You should welcome it. With feedback, you can learn how to shine at your job.

Rae works in a lab that makes false teeth. Rae's boss watches over her work and sometimes corrects what she is doing. Rae understands that her boss is just making sure the product is made correctly. She knows her boss is not picking on her.

All workers get negative feedback. You need to learn to accept it. You can use it to correct problems and learn to do a better job. But you should also accept positive feedback about what you are doing right. Take pride in what you've done well. Remember that your boss gives you constructive feedback to help you improve. In this lesson, you will learn strategies for getting and using feedback. You will also learn how to give feedback to others.

Sometimes feedback is given informally. Your boss may give feedback while you are working. Other times, you may get more formal feedback. You should always have the chance to respond to feedback. When you respond, remain calm and professional.

Handling Feedback

Feedback is a part of every job. It's important that you learn how to handle it well. Here are some basic guidelines.

Be objective. Don't get defensive about the suggestions your boss makes. You will get more from feedback if you keep an open mind. You'll find that your boss often makes a good point.

Don't take feedback personally. Feedback can be hard to hear. At times, it may seem insulting. Remember that feedback is based on your work behaviors. It's not personal.

Focus on what your supervisor is saying. Getting feedback can be stressful. It's natural to feel nervous. But don't let your nerves get in the way of hearing the feedback. Take a deep breath. Don't be afraid to ask your boss to repeat or explain details.

Use feedback to improve your work. Think about the feedback. How can you use it to improve your work? If you are not clear about this, ask your supervisor. Small changes can often make a big difference.

Below are examples of the types of informal feedback you might receive at work:

▶ informal one-on-one meetings with a supervisor
▶ team meetings or conferences
▶ notes (handwritten or typed)
▶ computer-generated reports
▶ e-mailed remarks

Keep an open mind. Try to see your boss's point of view. The feedback you get may help you to do your job better.

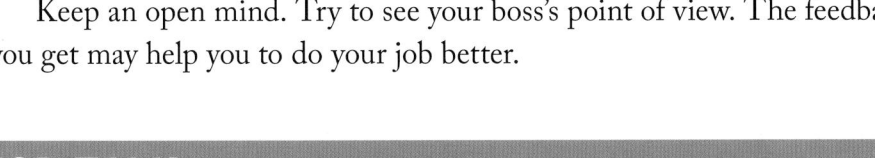

JOB TALK

Listening Through Stress

Getting feedback can be stressful. This can make it hard to listen carefully. Because of this, you may want to use these listening strategies. They can help you understand, remember, and use the feedback you receive.

Start by keeping eye contact with your supervisor. This will help you stay focused on what he or she is saying. Also, try repeating your supervisor's words in your head. This may help you remember what you are hearing. It may also help you decide whether you need to ask for something to be repeated.

You may find it helpful to take notes. Your notes will help you focus on the information you hear. You can read your notes later to remember all that was said. Writing down feedback can also make it seem less personal.

Giving Feedback

You have learned how to receive feedback at work. You may also have to give feedback. You may give feedback to your co-workers. Or maybe your boss. You can use much of what you've learned about getting feedback when you need to give it.

First, you should always be professional when giving feedback. Focus on the job performance. Don't let personal feelings or opinions affect your judgment. Consider the point of view of your co-worker when giving feedback.

Suppose your boss asks you to give feedback to your co-worker Mike. You and Mike both work at a local park. Mike has a good attitude about doing most jobs. However, he complains whenever you ask him to help clean up litter and garbage.

Use this form to give feedback to Michael:

I appreciate how you _____,

but you need to improve _____.

Keep these tips in mind when giving feedback to your supervisor. But also keep in mind that you are speaking to your boss. It is important to treat him respectfully. For example, a hospital worker might say to his boss, "It takes me a long time to see all my patients. I think it would help if I got more training on the new blood pressure machine."

JOB TALK

The Real Story

At times, your boss may give you an assignment that you think is unfair. But you may not know all the information your boss knew when she planned the work. As a result, her instructions may seem to make no sense. You may not agree with your boss's decision.

Your first instinct might be to get upset. Instead, try to get more information from your boss. This can help you to see the big picture. It can help you think like your boss. Read the following scene. Notice how Armando speaks to his boss. He starts with a positive statement, and then he adds his feedback.

SARAH, CUSTOMER

"You have to be finished and out of my house in two days. If you are not, I'm not going to pay you!"

BOB, OWNER OF CONTRACTING FIRM

"Jim, I need your guys to finish the job in two days."

JIM, CONTRACTOR

"Armando, I need you to finish laying the bathroom tile tonight."

ARMANDO, TILE LAYER

"I know we need to please the customer. But I do my best work when I have time to lay tile neatly. I need to make sure that it is straight."

What information could Jim, the contractor, have given Armando to help him understand his request better?

Now You Try It ...

Read the following scene about Angie and her boss, Clyde. Think about the information Clyde should have shared with Angie. Then answer the question.

Clyde is the manager of an auto repair shop. He gets a last-minute request from a local school district to repair one of their buses. Clyde knows this could lead to more work in the future. He asks one of his best mechanics, Angie, to work on her day off.

Clyde doesn't explain why he wants Angie to come in. Angie isn't happy about having to work on her day off. She needs to know more information.

What should Angie say to Clyde? Remember that Angie should always be respectful to her boss.

Job & Life Skills

Feedback or Gossip?

To be a good employee, you need feedback from the people you respect and trust at work. Feedback can help you improve the way you do your job. It can help you reach your goals. Your self-esteem can soar when you set and reach your goals.

However, some comments may harm your ability to reach your goals. Harmful comments, such as gossip (mean talk about others), can lower your confidence. It can hurt your reputation, or the way people think of you. Whenever possible, avoid harmful talk. Instead, focus on your goals.

The following activities will help you deal with co-workers' comments. After reading each activity, use the questions to start a group discussion.

Activity

Office Gossip

Sarah and Ami like to sit and complain about co-workers who walk by. Today, they are focused on Tanh. Tanh is one of the best workers in their office.

Every job has people like Sarah and Ami. They find something bad to say in every situation. Often, people who gossip about others have low self-esteem. In order to feel better about themselves, they talk poorly of others. At times, they may focus on people they think are threats to their own success.

Here are tips that will help you avoid negative talk at work.

1. Avoid gossip. When people try to spread gossip, ignore them.

2. Do not let gossip affect your work. Focus on your goals—not negative talk.

3. If work gossip and mean comments continue, report them to your supervisor. Ask for advice.

Think About It

1. Have you ever been the subject of gossip at work? If so, how did you react to it? How did others react to it?

2. What happened then?

3. What might you do if people gossip about you in the future?

Accept Feedback

Sometimes co-workers will give you feedback. By giving feedback, they are trying to help you do your job better. Like you, they want what's best for the company. You should attempt to use the feedback to improve your work. Use it to become the best worker you can be!

Read and discuss the script below. Then answer the questions.

Shannon:	Hey Gina—do you have enough hangers for those shirts?
Gina:	Yes, I think I have enough. This shipment just came in. The boss wants them hung up before I leave today.
Shannon:	I'm glad we're finally getting some fall clothes in stock. Remember that we need to put the shirts with flowers on the left. The solid colors go on the right.
Gina:	I didn't know we had to group the shirts that way! No one ever told me. How come no one told me about this?
Shannon:	I'm sorry. I thought you knew about the new display.
Gina:	I can't do my job right if I don't get the proper training.
Shannon:	I'm sorry. I didn't mean to upset you. I'm just trying to help.
Gina:	Well, thanks for your help. And I'm sorry too. I didn't mean to be rude. I just get frustrated when I don't know all of the store rules.
Shannon:	No problem, Gina. If you ever have any questions about anything, just ask. Now where did I put that color chart?

Think About It

1. Have you ever been in a situation like this? If so, how did you react to it?

2. What happened then?

3. What might you do when you are given feedback by a co-worker in the future?

Answer the questions. Use your answers to discuss your experiences with the class.

Performance Reviews

TERMS

merit raise a raise in pay a worker earns because of outstanding job performance

cost-of-living raise a small raise in pay that helps workers to pay for basic needs

disciplinary action a process used to correct an employee who breaks work rules

A year ago, Suzanne Boone began her job in a research lab. Last week, her boss told her it was time for her first annual (yearly) performance review.

Like Suzanne, most workers have formal reviews at least once a year. Employers often use these reviews to make decisions about jobs and pay.

Suzanne knew her boss would look at her skill at running tests and doing other tasks. She hoped she would earn an "exceeds expectations" rating. This would be a higher rating than "meets expectations." Getting the higher rating would mean that she is doing her job better than her boss expected. That rating could also mean than she gets a raise.

Workers who get great performance reviews are more likely to receive merit raises. A **merit raise** is a raise in pay that a worker earns because of outstanding job performance.

A worker who earns a lower rating might get just a cost-of-living raise. A **cost-of-living raise** is a small raise in pay that covers only basic needs such as the rising costs of food, clothing, and housing.

You may not always get a pay raise when you get a performance review. Some years, a company may not be able to afford to give a pay raise.

You may not agree with every score on your performance review. You have the right to explain why you disagree. Just remember to be calm and professional.

Performance Reviews

Good employees should be happy to have performance reviews. A review gives you a chance to get helpful feedback on your work. A review is a formal record of how well you do your job. Supervisors are often required to give performance reviews once a year.

Your performance review should not contain any surprises. Your boss should be giving you feedback regularly. Most of the time, your review will have information you already know.

A performance review starts with facts such as the worker's name, title, and the time period covered by the review.

Performance Review

Employee: Brandy Jackson
Title: Teacher Aide
Review Period: 2013-2014 Academic Year
Date of Review: 6/5/14

JOB SKILLS
Brandy has worked hard to increase her job skills this year. She has become a valued member of our staff. Her high standards set her apart from many of her peers.

WORK RESULTS
Brandy's work results are overall quite good. The test scores of many of the students she works with have improved. At times, she could enforce classroom rules better. This would help prevent bad behavior among students.

COMMUNICATION
Brandy has great verbal communication skills. She does very well when speaking face-to-face with co-workers, students, and parents. In the next year, she should focus on improving her written communication skills.

These are the areas in which Brandy was evaluated.

Brandy's supervisor wrote descriptions of her performance in each area.

PERFORMANCE EVALUATION

Employee: Alejandro Gomez
Title: Sales Associate
Review Period: 11/19/12 to 11/19/13
Date of Review: 11/21/13

This review lists the areas in which Alejandro was evaluated.

This form uses number scores from 4 (excellent) to 1 (poor) to rate Alejandro's performance.

	4 Excellent	3 Good	2 Average	1 Poor
Quality of Work		X		
Dependability (is reliable)		X		
Punctuality (is on time)			X	
Teamwork	X			
Initiative (has the drive to do things without being told)	X			
Communication			X	
Job Knowledge		X		

Steps for Disciplinary Action

Disciplinary action is used to correct a worker who has broken work rules. Have you heard someone say "I was written up"? When a supervisor "writes someone up," he makes a written report. The report includes what the worker did wrong and the disciplinary action taken to correct the worker.

Disciplinary actions are meant to help a worker grow and improve. If a problem behavior does not change, a worker could lose his job.

STEP BY STEP

This chart shows the steps that could be taken for disciplinary action. The steps used at your company will be described in your policy manual.

Employee breaks company policy.

For serious problems, such as stealing, lying, fighting, or carelessness, employee is fired.

Disciplinary action is taken to correct problem.

Employee receives a verbal warning about behavior.

Problem behavior continues.

Employee corrects behavior.

Employee receives a written warning.

Employee does not complete plan and is fired.

Employee begins a performance-improvement plan.

Employee completes plan, but behavior continues.

Company gives a final written warning. Employee is put on suspension (forced to stop working for a time).

Employee completes plan and corrects behavior.

Employee returns from suspension and corrects behavior.

Employee returns, but behavior continues.

Employee is fired.

Know the Terms

Read the terms and definitions in the table to the right. Then show you understand the terms by writing sentences or questions using the terms.

Example: The man was <u>terminated</u> for being <u>tardy</u> 15 days last month.

DISCIPLINE-RELATED TERMS

Term	Definition
Employment at will	A company can fire an employee at any time without a reason
Excessive absences	Missing work more than the number of days allowed by company policy
Fraud	Dishonest behavior (may also be illegal)
Gross negligence	Extreme carelessness or failure to do a job
Insubordination	Disrespecting authority or not doing what people in power say to do
Negligence	Failing to do a job
Tardiness	Arriving late
Termination	The ending of employment; firing
Theft	Taking property from its owner
Violence	The use of physical force in order to hurt or threaten another person

JOB LAW

Right-to-Work States

A labor union is an organization of workers that protects the rights of its members. Some jobs have labor unions and some do not. In some jobs, workers are required to join the union, if there is one. In Right-to-Work states, workers do not have to join a union, even if there is one.

If your job requires or offers union membership, learn all that you can about it. This will help you decide whether to join.

JOB LAW

Fair or Unfair?

At some time, you may get a performance evaluation or disciplinary action that you think is unfair. If you do, take time to look at the situation. Think honestly. Move past your hurt feelings.

If you still think you were treated unfairly, there are steps you can take. Check with your union, if you are a member. There may be guidelines to follow. Your union contract should explain what you need to do.

If you are not in a union, write out why you think the evaluation or disciplinary action was unfair. Use facts to back up your statements. Don't be emotional. Then show what you have written to your supervisor. Discuss the concerns you have.

If your supervisor is not willing to help, check your policy manual. It should explain the next steps to take.

Check off the goals you achieved in Chapter 3.

In Lesson 1, you . . .

☐ Learned how self-esteem can affect your work

☐ Wrote about the successes that build your self-esteem

☐ Planned to build your self-esteem at work

In Lesson 2, you . . .

☐ Learned how feedback is helpful at work

☐ Read about strategies for using feedback to improve your work

☐ Practiced giving feedback

In Lesson 3, you . . .

☐ Learned about performance reviews and how they can help you

☐ Read about common steps for disciplinary action

☐ Learned about labor unions

What do you want to know more about?

List the things that you want to learn more about. Talk to your teacher or look them up online.

_____

_____

Choose the best answer.

1. Employers show that they value their employees by

   A. spending time and money to train them.

   B. giving them negative feedback.

   C. organizing labor unions.

2. When you get feedback in the workplace, you should

   A. get defensive and argue with your supervisor.

   B. use it to improve your work.

   C. take it personally and feel insulted.

3. When giving feedback in the workplace, you should

   A. think only about your personal feelings.

   B. be friendly and casual.

   C. focus on performance.

True or false? If the statement is true, write *T*. If the statement is false, write *F*. Then change the false statement to make it true.

4. You can build self-esteem in the workplace by setting goals for yourself.

   _____

5. Performance reviews do not affect workers' wages or salaries.

   _____

Write your answer on the lines.

6. What are some important tips to remember when giving feedback to a supervisor?

   _____

   _____

Match the term on the left to the correct definition on the right.

7. disciplinary action   A. a feeling of pride and confidence in yourself

8. self-esteem   B. an increase in pay based on good job performance

9. labor union   C. an organization of workers that protects their rights

10. merit raise   D. a process used to correct a worker who breaks rules

The Diverse Workplace

GOALS

▶ THINK ABOUT diversity at work

▶ READ examples of discrimination and harassment

▶ STUDY discrimination and harassment policies

TERMS

diverse made up of things or people that are different from each other

gender a person's sex, either male or female

ethnicity group of people with the same customs, language, religion, etc.

cultural sensitivity an awareness of the various backgrounds of others

When you are hired, you join a team of co-workers. This team could be just a few people. It could also be a large group. No matter its size, everyone on this team should be working toward the same goals.

You may all be working toward common goals, but you will not all be alike. In fact, most workplaces are diverse. Something that is **diverse** is made up of things that are different from each other. A diverse workplace includes people of different beliefs, ages, genders, and backgrounds. **Gender** refers to a person's sex, either male or female.

All jobs are open to people of diverse races and ethnicities. People who have the same **ethnicity** have the same customs, language, religion, etc.

The people you work with may be very different from the people in your home life. They may be much older than you or belong to another race. It is important that you learn to work well with all sorts of people. When all workers act like professionals, they can get the job done.

The bar graph below shows the diversity found in different types of jobs.

Diverse Careers

Each bar represents 100% of the people who have that type of job.

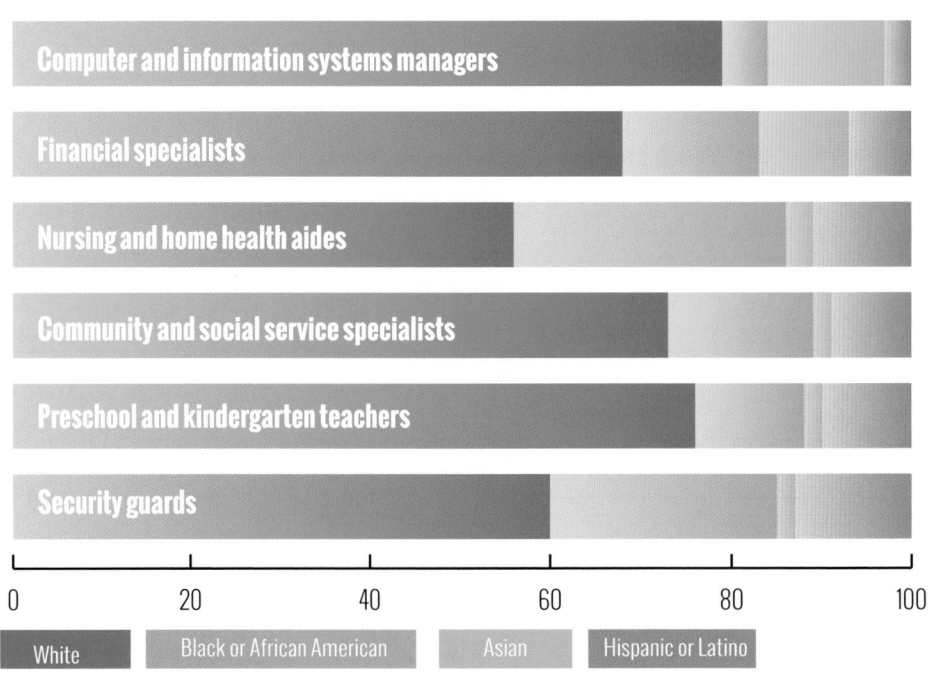

Source: Bureau of Labor Statistics, 2011

Cultural Sensitivity

At work, you should show **cultural sensitivity.** Cultural sensitivity is an awareness of the backgrounds of others. It means being aware of the ways these differences affect how others think and behave.

Cultural sensitivity means you accept how others may be different from you. Your company may offer training to help you be more culturally sensitive. It may give you a list of things to avoid saying or doing, such as:

▶ asking a co-worker, "Why do you eat such weird food?"
▶ telling jokes about groups of people
▶ making fun of someone who dresses in a way you find odd

Be careful what you say and do at work. At times, you might say something just because you are curious. Even so, your words could still offend someone.

Some issues might not be obvious. These could include sexual preference, religion, or political beliefs. If something could offend someone, it's best to not say or do it.

At times, you may be asked a question that offends you. If this happens, feel free to not answer it. You could try to change the subject. Or you may decide to answer it. This would give you a chance to explain why it was offensive.

JOB TALK

Change the Subject

You can show respect for diversity at work in many ways. You can listen, show kindness, and treat others fairly.

But you can't control what your co-workers say and do. If a co-worker brings up an offensive topic, you should ignore the remark. Then quickly change the subject. Think of safe topics. Traffic and the weather are good ones.

This sends a clear message to a co-worker. You can also steer the conversation toward work. Remember: If a subject is not work related, it probably should not be discussed.

Activity

Working Together

Think about some of your job, school, or volunteer experiences. Were there times when you worked with people who were different from you? Use these experiences to answer the questions below.

1. How did other people's backgrounds differ from your own?

2. What steps did you take so you could work well with them?

Good employees act professionally. Acting professionally means treating all co-workers fairly.

Discrimination

Most companies try to be open and safe places for all their workers. One way they can do this is through discrimination rules. Discrimination is when a person or group is not treated fairly based on one or more of their differences. Some types of discrimination include:

▶ age
▶ gender
▶ race
▶ ethnic background
▶ religious beliefs
▶ political beliefs
▶ social status (how much one earns and how one lives)

The men in this office are leaving Kelly out because she is a woman. This is gender discrimination.

Company rules protect employees from discrimination. Federal laws do too. The Civil Rights Act of 1964 bans discrimination. The Equal Employment Opportunity Commission (EEOC) works to make sure the laws are followed.

It is against the law to give men and women different pay for the same work. Other laws protect workers from discrimination because of age or disabilities.

Both federal laws and company rules give workers ways to complain about discrimination. If you believe you're being discriminated against, check these laws and rules to learn about ways to correct the problem.

Study the examples on page 81. They tell about ways in which discrimination may happen at work.

CHARGES OF EMPLOYER DISCRIMINATION IN THE U.S.

This graph shows the numbers of employer discrimination charges filed by workers. Each charge may include more than one type of discrimination.

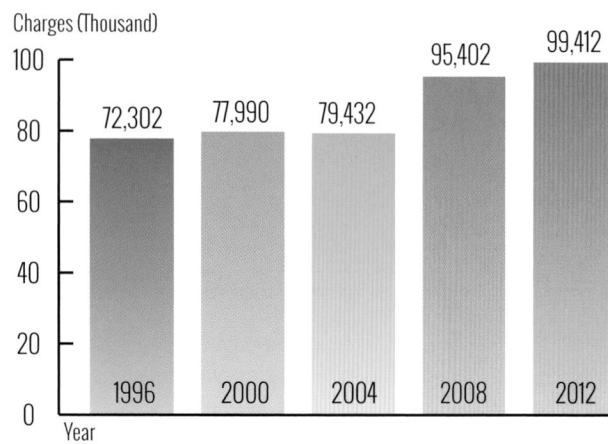

Charges (Thousand)

Year	Charges
1996	72,302
2000	77,990
2004	79,432
2008	95,402
2012	99,412

TYPES OF EMPLOYEE DISCRIMINATION CHARGES

This table lists the most common types of discrimination charges that workers report.

TYPE	NUMBER OF CHARGES	% OF TOTAL CHARGES
Retaliation—all types	37,836	38.1%
Race	33,512	33.7%
Gender	30,356	30.5%
Disability	26,379	26.5%
Age	22,857	23.0%
National origin	10,883	10.9%
Religion	3,811	3.8%

Source: U.S. EEOC

Examples of Discrimination

1. Gender

A male boss gives the most important tasks to male workers. He gives female workers small tasks that are less important. This boss is discriminating against employees who are female.

2. Ethnic background

A white supervisor rarely speaks with his new worker, Pedro, who is from Mexico. When he gives the other workers job information, he does not tell Pedro. This boss is discriminating against Pedro because of his ethnicity.

3. Religion

One boss gives extra shifts to workers who go to his church. The workers who do not go to his church get fewer chances for overtime. This boss is discriminating against employees who do not share his religious beliefs.

4. Age

An older worker is often left out of group projects. His co-coworkers hold meetings without him. These workers are discriminating against a man because of his age.

Activity

Discrimination Policy

Read this sample of a discrimination policy. Then answer the questions. Write your answers on paper or discuss them in class.

1. What do you think the phrase "equal opportunity employer" means?

2. Would a manager at Jones Books be able to give a worker a raise based on his or her race?

3. Jones Books does not make decisions about hiring workers based on what characteristics?

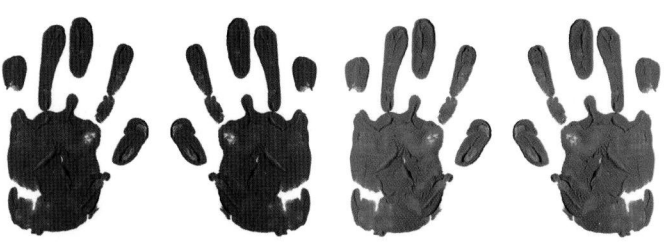

Anti-Discrimination Policy

Jones Books is an equal opportunity employer. Jones Books will not discriminate. Jones Books will act to prevent all discrimination.

There will be no discrimination in:

- employment
- hiring
- promotions
- pay
- termination

There will be no discrimination of any employee or potential employee based on:

- race
- ethnicity
- religion
- sexual preference
- gender

Harassment

You first learned about harassment in Chapter 1. Harassment is conduct that disturbs or upsets another worker. Employers have rules to prevent harassment. When harassment involves sexual comments or actions, it is called sexual harassment.

People at work come from different backgrounds. A comment or an action may seem harmless to you. But it may offend someone else. A person's age, ethnic background, and gender will affect what he thinks is OK and not OK.

Harassment includes a wide range of behaviors. Here are a few:

- ▶ threats
- ▶ bullying
- ▶ sexual comments
- ▶ insults
- ▶ aggressive behavior

As an employee, you must recognize harassment so you can avoid it. When it comes to harassment, it doesn't matter if you mean to offend someone. The only thing that matters is the way your behavior affects the other person.

Study the examples on page 83. They show ways in which harassment may happen at work.

Touching a co-worker can be harassment. You may be comfortable putting your hand on a friend's arm. But this could make a co-worker uncomfortable. Remember to behave like a professional at work.

HARASSMENT CHARGES RECEIVED BY U.S. EEOC & FAIR EMPLOYMENT PRACTICES AGENCIES

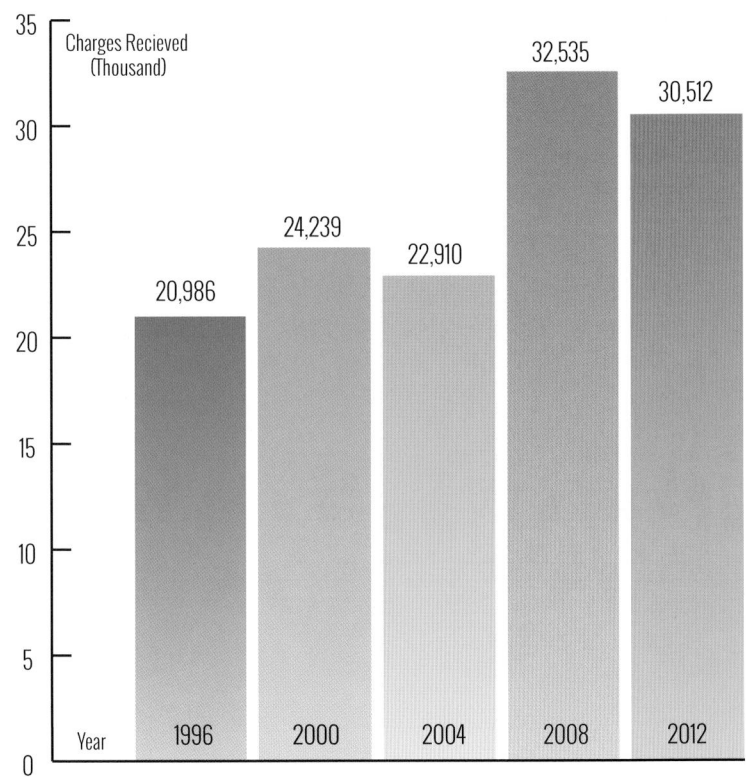

The national EEOC works to resolve charges of harassment at work.

Charges Recieved (Thousand)

Year	1996	2000	2004	2008	2012
Charges	20,986	24,239	22,910	32,535	30,512

Source: U.S. EEOC

Examples of Harassment

1. Offensive Comments

A worker loudly reads a joke that makes fun of women. Many of his co-workers are women. This is workplace harassment.

2. Inappropriate Behavior

A male worker asks a female co-worker to go on a date with him. She turns him down. He keeps asking her to go out. He sends her flowers at work. This pushy behavior makes the woman uncomfortable. This is sexual harassment.

3. Comments about a Person's Body

A female employee asks a male employee to show his muscles to her. This comment is meant to be funny. But it can be seen as offensive. Some actions may be OK in a social setting, but not at work. This is harassment.

4. Hostile or Mean Behavior

A group of workers of one race threatens a worker of another race. They threaten to damage his car. This type of hostile behavior is harassment based on race.

Activity

Harassment Policy

Read this sample of a harassment policy. Then answer the questions. Write your answers on paper or discuss them in class.

1. How would you describe Smith Shoes' attitude toward harassment?

2. What are some of the ways Smith Shoes may deal with harassment?

3. What factors might Smith Shoes look at when dealing with a harassment complaint?

Harassment Policy

Smith Shoes does not allow harassment. Complaints are taken very seriously.

Employees responsible for harassment may be subject to the following actions:

- training
- counseling
- disciplinary action
- loss of promotion or raise
- job reassignment
- suspension
- termination of employment

Where Are You Going?

GOALS

▶ WRITE a list of short- and long-term goals

▶ LEARN the steps for earning a raise or promotion

▶ READ about how to leave one job and accept another

TERMS

promotion a move up to a better position

corporate structure the way in which a company's jobs and departments are organized

résumé a short document describing your education, work history, and skills

Deon Rogers worked as a store clerk. He'd been working for six months. In that time, he had quickly learned the skills he needed for his job. He felt he knew his job well. In fact, he'd begun to seek out other duties to do around the store.

Rogers decided that he would like a **promotion** to the position of manager. When a worker gets a promotion, he is moved up to a better position.

You may also want to be promoted. One of the first steps is to understand your place in your company. To do this, you must look at the company's corporate structure. A **corporate structure** is the way in which a company's jobs and departments are organized. By looking at corporate structure, you can see which positions you might move up to.

You may see that the jobs open to you are limited. If so, you may decide to seek out more training. You may also decide to look for a job with another business.

Study the two charts shown below. They show the corporate structures of a retail company and a medical lab.

> *A salesperson in this company could move up to become Retail Operations Manager.*

> *To move up in this lab, a technician would need to earn a bachelor's degree.*

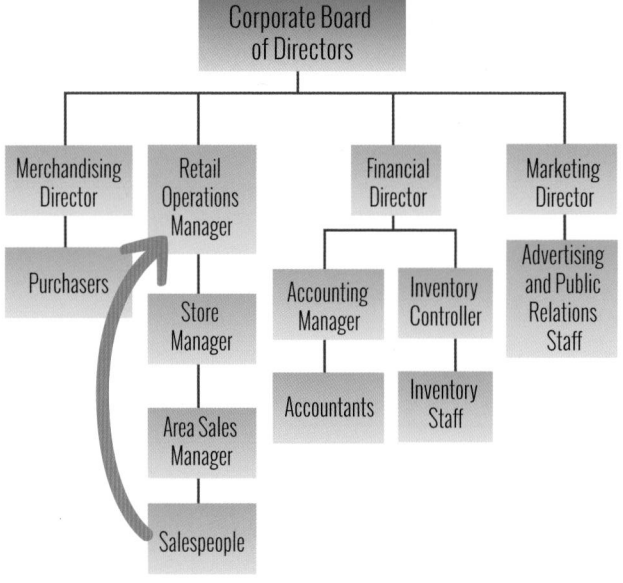

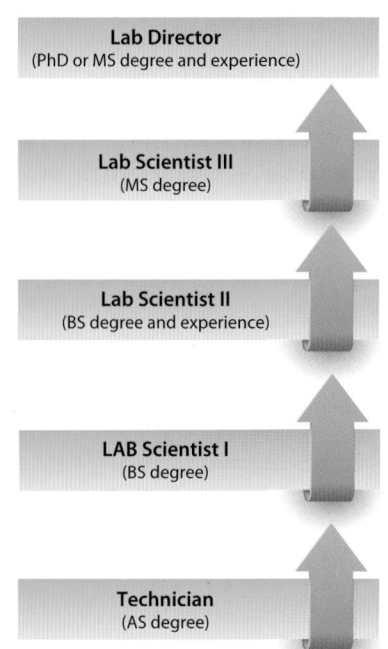

What Are Your Goals?

In the space below, write your goals. Think of short-term goals that you can reach in three months. Think of long-term goals that you might reach in one year. Also, think about some five-year goals for the future.

As you think about these, try to match your personal goals with your work goals. Suppose you want to buy a car. Think about how much money you would need to earn to pay for it. This information may affect your career goals.

3 MONTHS

Personal: _____

Work: _____

Get a certificate in computer repair

1 YEAR

Personal: _____

Work: _____

Get promoted to shift supervisor

5 YEARS

Personal: _____

Work: _____

Earn my bachelor's degree

JOB & LIFE SKILLS

Balancing Work and Life

All employees have to balance their work tasks with their daily lives. Sometimes your personal life keeps you from reaching a career goal. Your goal could be a promotion, a raise, or even a new job. Having no car may stop you from work travel. Child care needs may stop you from working more or different hours.

Remember that these issues may only be temporary. Child care needs may affect the hours you can work. Think ahead to when your kids start school. At that point, you may be able to change your schedule.

Try to look ahead when thinking of your career goals. This way, you can plan for the future. You may need extra training or to go back to school. What you want may not happen right away. If you stay positive and focused, you can reach your goals.

Promotion Plan

You've made both short-term and long-term goals. Now it's time to create a plan for promotion. In some cases, a promotion may require you to go to school. You will learn about getting more education in Lesson 3.

In other cases, you may need to show you have mastered your present job. Doing your job very well can sometimes help you earn a promotion, a raise in pay, or a higher pay grade. A pay grade is the level of pay you can make for the work you do. Read the flowchart below to see some tips that you can use to create your own promotion plan.

Steps to Earn a Promotion

1. Begin to work toward a promotion as soon as you start a new job. Ask your supervisor or a mentor about the skills you need to get ahead in the company.

2. Set goals to learn new skills. Look at the skills you need for your job. Which skills do you need to work on? Take advantage of chances to learn and practice these skills.

3. Check on your progress. Look at the steps you've already taken. Don't be too hard on yourself. Keep working to reach your goals.

4. To be successful, look and act like you already are. Be professional. This will help you earn a good name at work. Companies promote workers who are skillful, dependable, and worthy of trust.

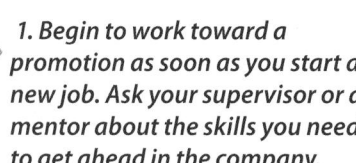

5. Volunteer for new responsibilities. Doing so will show you always work to do your best. It will show you are able to handle more than one task at once. It proves you are a valuable employee.

6. Work well with your mentor. A mentor can tell others about your work. You can also learn from your mentor's own experiences about being promoted.

8. Be a team player. Working well as part of a team can boost your chances for a raise or a new position.

7. Develop a good relationship with your boss. Take opportunities to show your skills. Make sure your boss sees how well you do your job.

9. Write down the work you do and your successes. Sharing these positive results will help you when you ask for a promotion.

Moving On

At some point, you may decide that your next step is to change jobs. Perhaps you can't move up any further in your company. You may have learned the skills you need for a better job somewhere else. No matter why you are leaving, it's important to look for a new job in the right way.

Before you leave your job, find out your employer's rules about any pay and benefits your company owes you. Find out if you've earned any sick or vacation time you have not used. Ask what you need to do about it.

You should also ask about your health care plan. You may not be covered by your new employer's health care plan right away. If this is so, you can keep your present plan through a program called COBRA. It lasts for the time between jobs or until you join a new health care plan. It is expensive, but it will keep you covered until your new health care plan starts.

Write down your supervisor's name and contact information. Do this for the human resource person, too. You may need this information for your résumé or a future job application. A **résumé** is a short document describing your education, job skills, and work history. You give it to an employer when you are applying for a job.

JOB TALK

Saying Goodbye

Leaving a job is not easy. But it can be easier if you behave like a professional as you prepare to leave.

First, you should give your employer notice that you plan to leave. Notice is a warning or statement that an employee is leaving. In most cases, people try to give notice at least two weeks before they leave.

After giving notice, you should also write a letter of resignation. This is a letter telling that you are leaving your job. Keep it short and simple. Don't try to explain your reasons for leaving.

Thank your employer for the opportunities you had on the job. Try to keep a good relationship with your employer. This can help you if you need a reference in the future. When someone gives you a job reference, he tells a possible employer about your job performance. You may wish to ask your boss to give you a job reference before you leave.

Remain professional while leaving your job. Stay on good terms with your co-workers. You never know when you might meet them again.

GOALS

▶ LEARN the types of education you may need to reach your goals

▶ READ about the ways employers help workers learn new skills

▶ LEARN how to update your résumé

TERMS

intern a student who works at a job to get experience

A Better You

You are always learning and improving your skills on the job.

But you may need more training to reach your goals or to earn a promotion. At times, you may need more training in order to keep your job.

For example, some child care workers must take classes. They need to be certified. They must continue to take classes to keep their certification from year to year. Some must also become certified in first aid.

In some cases, an employer pays for or helps pay for classes. In other cases, workers pay for their classes.

Study the diagram below. It shows an example of what one worker did to move up in her job.

Continuing Education = Success

Paloma works with health care records. She has an associate's degree in Health Information Technology.

Paloma continues her education. She takes management training classes.

Paloma continues to take classes. She is working to earn her Registered Health Information Technician (RHIT) certificate.

Paloma earns a bachelor's degree in Computer Information Systems. She is promoted to health information manager.

Paloma takes classes to work with cancer records.

Paloma wants to learn the newest information about her job. She takes advanced computer classes.

How to Reach Your Goals

Jennifer, Maylea, and DeSean have made some career goals. Read the steps they have taken to reach them. Use the steps as a guide for your own planning.

Jennifer wants to start a cake decorating business.

- She decides to work from her home. She tells friends about her plans and looks for customers.

- She looks into the types of funding (money help) open to women who want to start a small business.

- She gets business advice. She wants to know the risks of starting a business.

Maylea works as a dental assistant. She wants to become a dental hygienist.

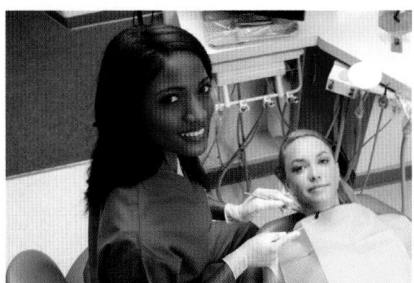

- She plans how to go to dental hygiene school.

- She works out a schedule so she can go to school and work at the same time.

- She needs a certificate or a degree in dental hygiene.

- She must pass a licensing exam in her home state.

DeSean wants to become a police officer.

- He looks up the job requirements of his local police department. He decides to take a course in law enforcement.

- He looks online and finds the course at his local community college.

- He signs up for a gym membership. Police officers need to be in top physical shape.

- He learns that many police departments are looking for officers who speak a second language. He signs up for a Spanish class.

Review the five-year goals you set for yourself in Lesson 2. What types of training, certification, or degrees will you need? What other things will you need to do? List all the steps to reaching your goals.

After you have listed your steps, use the Internet for more research. Find answers to questions such as these:

- Where can you find the training you need in your local area?

- How long will these steps take?

- How much they will they cost?

Use this information to revise your goals. Make a 10-year career goal.

Notes: _____

_____

_____

10-YEAR GOAL: _____

_____

_____

_____

Employer Assistance

Many employers encourage their workers to improve their work skills. When employees work better, the company does better too. Employers support their workers in several ways. They may:

- ▶ provide their own training
- ▶ help to pay for training
- ▶ adjust work schedules so workers can take classes
- ▶ provide training outside of work

You can learn skills and get good experience from every job you have. Take advantage of any chance to learn new skills. Volunteer to lead projects or groups. These experiences can help you improve your leadership skills.

First Aid and CPR/AED Certification

Some employers offer a class for learning first aid and CPR/AED. CPR/AED (cardiopulmonary resuscitation and automated external defibrillator) training teaches life-saving skills.

Professional Development

Many workers sign up for training to learn new methods, equipment, and rules. They use training to keep up with changes in their jobs. Many employers will pay for this training.

Tuition Help

At times, you may choose to take a class on your own. Some classes cost money. You may have to pay tuition or a fee. If the class helps you do your job, your employer may pay some or all of the fee.

Technology changes quickly. Continuing education is the best way to keep your skills up to date.

Your Résumé

The résumé you make while looking for a job should not stay the same for long. Every month or so, you should update it. You should include new certificates, skills, and training you've gotten on your job. It will be easier if you update your résumé regularly. If you wait, you may not remember all that you've learned and done.

Here is an example of a résumé and how to update it. The notes on the left include ideas of things to add and where to add them.

I was in charge of a group that figured out which new software to buy.

• List this skill under Experience. Leadership skills are useful for any job.

I got my associate's degree so I could be a Web designer.

• Place this information under Education. Make sure that you correctly list and describe the degrees or certificates you receive.

I know how to use a lot of computer design programs.

• List this under Skills/Certifications. Here you can list skills that may not directly relate to your work experience.

KIANNA A. BROOKS

18930 68th Ave. NE, Apt 1107
Kenmore, WA 98028-2663
(425) 545-5555
brooks_ca@pax.com

Summary of Qualifications
Experienced customer support specialist experienced in diagnosing and resolving a variety of problems associated with computer hardware and software.

Experience
Customer Support Assistant, September 2010 to Present
Watersource, Inc., Bothell, WA
- **Led a research group that analyzed and purchased software for the company**
- Monitor performance of company networks and resolve technical issues that arise

Volunteer Help-Desk Technician, June 2010 to September 2010
Specialty Products, Inc., Kenmore, WA
- Responded to customer calls and e-mail requesting assistance using company website
- Determined problems and provided step-by-step instructions to help customers resolve issues

Education
Cascadia Community College, Bothell, WA
Associate Degree in Applied Science–
Web Application Programming Technology (May 2012)

Lynwood High School, Lynwood, WA
- High School diploma (June 2007)

Skills/Certifications
Specialized at troubleshooting local area network (LAN) and wide area network (WAN) problems

Proficient with Adobe® Photoshop®, Acrobat® and Illustrator®

Job Talk

Me in 10 Years...

Brandon is tired. He works during the day and takes classes at night. But it's worth it. Brandon wants to become a forensic scientist. One day, he hopes to be an expert in firearms and tool marks. Forensic scientists examine crime scene evidence for clues left by guns. They also identify tools used in a crime, such as those used for forcing open windows or doors.

Brandon left college for a while to get a full-time job. He needed to make money when he and his girlfriend had a baby. Today he's back in school. He takes evening classes part time to pursue his dream.

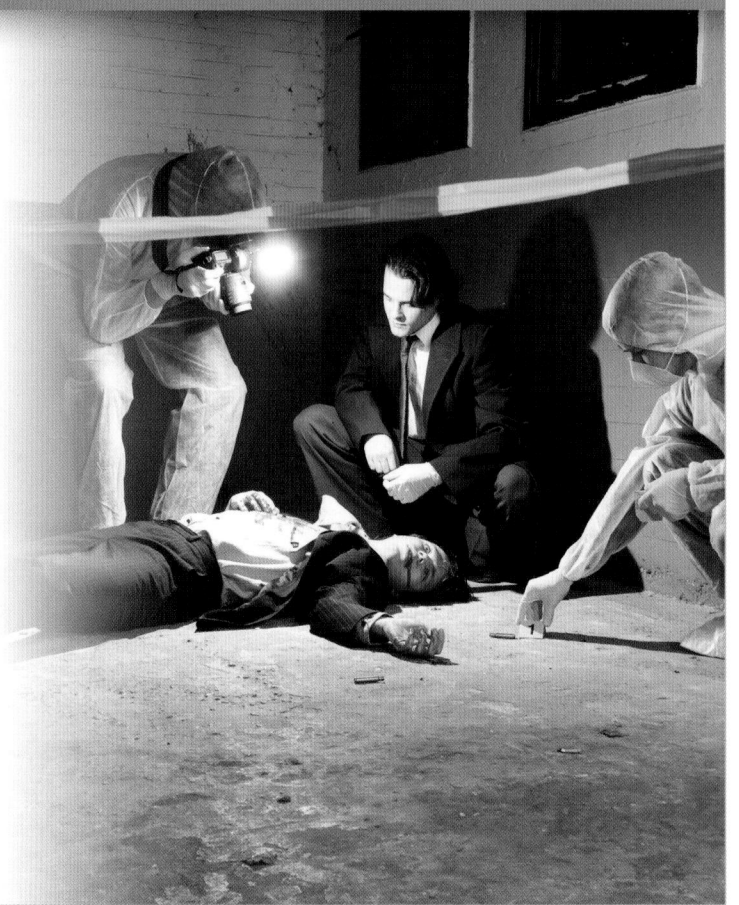

CRIME SCENE INVESTIGATOR

Currently, Brandon goes to a community college. Soon, he will earn his Associate in Science (AS) degree in crime scene technology. This will allow Brandon to work in a crime scene lab. He will earn more money in this new job than he does now as a store clerk.

Once Brandon has a job in a crime scene lab, he will continue with his education. With the extra pay of the new job, he will take his next set of classes. When he is through, he will earn a Bachelor of Science (BS) degree. This is what he needs to reach his goal. In the end, he will be a forensic scientist.

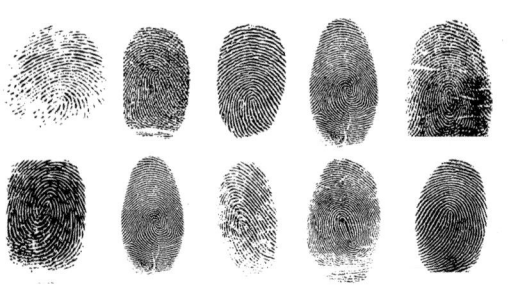

Activity

Read Brandon's 10-year plan. Then write your own 10-year plan in the table below. Some goals will take more than one year. Plan carefully.

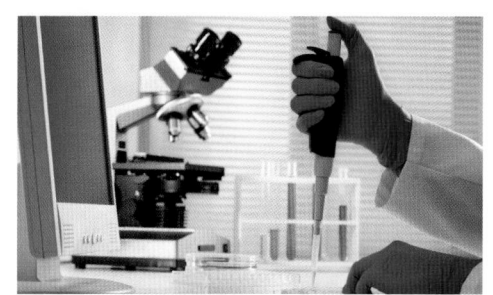

Brandon: Where I want to be in 10 years

Year	Goal	How will I do it? What will I need?
1	Brandon takes classes for his Associate of Science (AS) degree.	*Go to classes:* I need time and money.
2	Brandon works as an intern for his local police department's CSI unit.	*Work as an intern:* I need time.
3	Brandon works as an intern for the Bureau of Alcohol, Tobacco, and Firearms.	*Work as an intern:* I need time.
4	Brandon earns his AS degree and gets a job as a crime scene investigator.	*Finish my degree:* I need time and money. *Find a job:* I need time.
6	Brandon begins taking night classes to earn his Bachelor of Science (BS) degree in forensic science.	*Attend classes:* I need time and money.
9	Brandon completes his BS degree in forensic science and gets a job with a private forensics laboratory.	*Finish my degree:* I need time and money. *Find a job:* I need time.
10	Brandon becomes a certified firearms and tool mark examiner.	*Become certified:* I need time, and I need to pass tests.

Me in 10 Years

Year	Goal	How will I do it? What will I need?

Job Talk

PRESENT YOUR PLAN

You now have a 10-year plan. Use it to create and present a report to your class. You can use a program such as PowerPoint. If you are not familiar with this type of software, ask your teacher or a classmate for help.

Your report should include slides that show your job plan. Include at least one chart or graph and one photograph. Use the following tips to prepare your report:

- Research your career. You can use books, magazines, or web sites.

- Create tables, charts, or other graphics to support your information.

- Make sure your online sources are reliable. Use sites that end in .gov, .org, or .edu.

- Give your report in a professional manner.

These slides are from a presentation that Brandon might give. You may want to use them as models for your slides.

Show the sources you used to get your information. The Bureau of Labor Statistics has information about many jobs at www.bls.gov.

Use data to create a graph. This graph gives the expected employment data through 2018. It shows there will likely be a job for Brandon in the future.

Employment Projections 2010-2020
Projected increase in employment

Private detectives	21%
Forensic scientists	19%
Security guards	19%
Science technicians	11%
Police and detectives	7%

0 5 10 15 20 25

Source: U.S. Bureau of Labor Statistics

Use photos to show the duties that someone in your job must do.

Forensic Scientists at Work

Forensic scientists may be asked to speak in court as experts. They must be prepared to answer questions from lawyers about their knowledge of crime scenes.

Label your charts, graphs, and pictures with captions that explain them.

COSTS AND BENEFITS

Make a chart to show what it will cost to reach your goal and what the benefits will be. Be sure to include higher self-esteem and a sense of success.

Associate of Science degree—Crime Scene Technology
- *Costs:* $22,700; time away from family
- *Benefits:* Salary $32,000+; feeling of success; professional job

Bachelor of Science degree—Forensic Science
- *Costs:* $24,800; time away from family; schoolwork in addition to a full-time job
- *Benefits:* Salary $55,000+; feeling of success; professional job; higher self-esteem

Certification in Firearms and Tool Marks
- *Costs:* $250 for fees; time to study for tests
- *Benefits:* AFTE certification; I will be an expert; achievement of goals

Because Brandon goes to a college in his home state, he pays less than the out-of-state students pay.

Activity

Scoring Guide

Read this chart. It shows what you need to include in your report to get a good grade.

Grade	Guidelines for Presentation
Excellent	Includes: Graphs, photos, and pictures Data from reliable sources (sources are listed) Complete explanation of goal and steps to achieve goal Confident and smooth presentation style
Good	Includes: A graph and a photo Data from reliable sources (sources are listed) Good explanation of goal and steps to achieve goal Confident and smooth presentation style
Fair	Lacks graphs, but includes one picture Data comes from questionable sources Only brief explanation of goal and steps to achieve goal Awkward presentation style
Poor	Lacks graphs and pictures Data comes from unreliable sources Explanation of goal and steps to achieve goal are weak Poor presentation style

Selling Yourself, Again

GOALS

▶ LEARN how to promote your successes at work

▶ LEARN strategies for shyness

▶ THINK like a supervisor

TERMS

self-promotion telling others about your skills and successes

self-awareness knowing your own personality

When you're looking for a job, you must sell your skills to employers.
Once you get a job, you should continue to sell, or promote, yourself at work. **Self-promotion** means telling others about your skills and accomplishments or successes.

When you promote the good things about your work, you meet a few goals. Your bosses see you as successful and a good person for the job. Your co-workers see you as an honest, hard-working, and skilled worker.

Self-promotion needs to be done in the right way. You don't want to sound dishonest or boastful. Don't take credit for the work of others. Here are some tips for how to promote yourself at work:

▶ **Be ready to talk about your work.** When someone asks you how things are going, tell them. Mention something that has gone well.
▶ **Stick to the facts.** Tell about the goals you have met.
▶ **Write down your successes.** You can use this list during performance reviews.
▶ **Be enthusiastic.** Acting like you are excited about your work shows that you care.
▶ **Promote others.** Talking about your co-workers' accomplishments shows you are a team player.

Activity

Self-Promotion

These workers are promoting their successes. Circle the statements that show good ways of self-promotion. Draw an *X* over the statements that show poor ways of self-promotion.

> *"I am so excited! I got a perfect score on my training test!"*

> *"Hi, Felicia! Did you see I beat your sales record?"*

> *"Good thing I was at the meeting because Jessie really messed up."*

> *"I just opened my fifth credit account of the day!"*

Activity

Hey, Look at Me!

It is good to know how you are most comfortable promoting yourself. There are lots of ways. Here is a list to start with. Rate each one by your own comfort level. There are extra spaces to add others you've tried. Talk about this with others, and add more ideas.

Then make a personal plan for how you will share your work successes with your boss.

Ways I Can Sell Myself	Yes	Maybe	Maybe Not	No
Send an e-mail to my boss				
Send a written note				
Talk on the telephone				
Talk with my boss face-to-face				
Talk with my boss, along with a co-worker				
Show my boss a skill I have learned				
Share a picture of something I've made				
Share how my boss helped me improve				
Invite my boss to watch me work				
Show my boss how I work and ask for suggestions				

Strategies for Shyness

If you are shy, you are not alone. About 40 percent of Americans think of themselves as shy. At times, all people may act shy when they don't feel confident. It's natural to feel shy when facing a challenge, such as a new job. But there are ways you can overcome your shyness and reach your work goals.

One of the first steps to overcoming shyness is to be self-aware. **Self-awareness** means you know and understand your own personality. Notice the times when you feel shy. When you see a situation where you would normally feel shy, choose to speak up. It may be difficult at first. But with time, it will get easier. Stay strong and focus on your goal. You can overcome your shyness one day at a time.

What you have to say matters. Use the chances you get to tell about your ideas.

When you work to become more confident, you take a big step toward beating shyness. There are many ways to build your confidence.

▶ Give yourself extra time to prepare important tasks.

▶ Think more positively about the times you must interact with co-workers.

▶ Think of a company meeting as a time to get support. This may make it easier to speak up.

▶ Take small steps to become more open. Small steps will help you to slowly feel and act less shy.

Activity

Just a Note

Employees in many types of jobs need to communicate in writing. An aide in a nursing home may write a note about patient care. You may need to write notes to team members. You may need to write notes telling other workers what tasks you have completed.

Writing notes can also be a way for shy workers to communicate. If you are shy, you can write notes to your boss to tell of your successes.

Study these two examples. Then write a note to your teacher. Describe your successes over the past week.

I completed the virus check on your computer. I also installed new software.

Mrs. West ate very little dinner last night. She had a cold and went to sleep around 8:30 p.m.

Thinking Like a Supervisor

Thinking like a supervisor or manager can help you in several ways. You can begin to understand your supervisor's job. It might help you to be better prepared if you are promoted. It can help you improve in your current job. It can also help you to make a strong case for a future promotion.

If you were a supervisor, what traits would you look for in your employees? You might look for workers who are:

- punctual (on time)
- honest
- respectful
- dependable
- goal-driven

Start now and show these traits in your own work. Such behavior may lead to a promotion.

Managing Former Co-Workers

Getting a promotion is a wonderful thing. But a promotion can have some drawbacks. You may find that you're now the boss for your former co-workers. This can be awkward.

You may enjoy socializing with your co-workers. But what if you're now their boss? What if they know that you have made poor decisions in the past? This might cause them to lose respect for you as a boss. Without respect, it is very difficult for a supervisor to lead.

The best way to handle the situation is to stay professional. Do your best. Be honest and dependable. Treat your employees with respect.

Bill enjoys going to lunch with Chris, Jenna, and Eli. He always remembers to be professional.

Bill has always behaved in a professional manner. His co-workers respect him now that he is their boss.

Mentoring and Managing

GOALS

▶ LEARN how to mentor other employees at work

▶ STUDY the responsibilities of a manager

▶ PRACTICE management skills

TERMS

delegate to give control or responsibility to someone

motivation giving someone a good reason to want to do something

budget a plan for how to spend money

In Chapter 1, you learned that a mentor can help you when you are learning a new job. As you get more experienced in your job, you may get the chance to become a mentor yourself.

To learn how to become a mentor, think about the people who were mentors to you. What did you learn from them? What would you like to pass on to a new employee? How might you help a new worker find her way around? What job skills might you teach?

Mentors share information about their employers. They can help workers with their job challenges. They can offer tips for improving job skills. The checklist below gives some of the key talents of a good mentor.

When you are a mentor, you must behave as a professional. You will be helping a new worker succeed in his job. People often remember more about their mentors than they do about their bosses.

A Good Mentor …

▶ Is willing to give time to mentoring a new worker
▶ Is honest
▶ Has strong communication skills
▶ Is successful at work
▶ Works well with people from many backgrounds
▶ Is sensitive to others' feelings

Activity

Who Are Your Mentors?

Think about people who have been your mentors. They may be from your personal life or from jobs you have had. List what you have learned from your mentors. Then add ways in which you might have acted as a mentor to others.

Becoming a Mentor

Mentors are important to new employees. They set the tone at the new job. They pass on information and tips that can lead to job success.

A good mentor has a positive attitude. This can help new workers develop their own positive view. A good mentor should also have very good work skills.

JOB TALK

Active Listening

Think back to what you learned about active listening skills in Chapter 2. You can use these same skills when you are a mentor.

Use the following tips to become a better active listener:

1. **Listen** closely when a co-worker discusses a work problem with you. Don't interrupt. Let her finish speaking.

2. **Look** your co-worker in the eyes. This will show that you are listening.

3. **Pay attention** to your co-worker's body language. Look at the way he is sitting and his gestures. What do they tell you about how he is feeling?

4. **Respond** in ways that show that you understand. Nod your head as she speaks. When she has finished, restate what she said in your own words.

Management

Managers (bosses) are like mentors in some ways. They help workers do their best. They work to create a positive workplace.

Managers also have jobs that are quite different from mentors. They have more responsibilities than a mentor. They often must delegate tasks. When you **delegate,** you give someone the responsibility to do a job. Delegating gives workers the chance to grow. It puts them in control. It also lets managers see how well their workers can do.

Managers need great communication skills. They must give information to many people in the company. Good communication helps improve everyone's work. It also cuts down on confusion.

Strong managers should be well organized. They need to know the best ways to complete work tasks. They must schedule their employees. When making decisions, managers must think about what is best for the company.

A good manager makes sure that his workers are trained well for their jobs. Skilled workers are confident and perform their jobs well.

Activity

Be the Manager

A teacher is a kind of manager: a classroom manager. Suppose that you will manage this class for a week. Ask your teacher to give you a list of what needs to be taught. Using this information, plan the class activities for the week. Make sure that your plan covers everything: lessons, supplies, equipment, etc.

These are the types of decisions that managers make every day. They often have to make them on their own, without help from others.

_____

_____

_____

_____

_____

_____

Management Responsibilities

Andrew is a restaurant manager. He works with the restaurant's owner, employees, and customers. He has many roles and responsibilities.

OWNER
The owner is Andrew's boss. She expects Andrew to run the restaurant so it makes a profit (makes money). She provides him with sales goals. Andrew lets her know when he needs to spend money on staff or equipment.

CUSTOMER SERVICE
Some staff work for and with the customers. They give Andrew the feedback they hear from customers. He instructs staff on how to give excellent service.

KITCHEN
The chef, cooks, and dishwashers work in the kitchen. They let Andrew know how long it will take them to prepare orders. They tell him what supplies they will need. He guides them to prepare food and use the equipment safely.

RESTAURANT MANAGER, ANDREW
Andrew manages all the employees. He gets directions from the owner. He listens closely to his staff and the customers. He has to balance what he hears from everyone to make the restaurant run smoothly.

CUSTOMERS
Customer feedback is very important. Andrew takes all comments seriously. Sometimes he must act quickly to fix problems.

Management Challenges

Managers are often faced with challenges. Some companies give their managers high goals to meet. Managers then must figure out how to meet these goals.

Managers must work with all sorts of employees. Some may not be doing a good job. It is up to the manager to help them improve. A manager may try motivation or more training. **Motivation** means giving a person a good reason to want to do something. Sometimes managers must use disciplinary action (see page 74). When workers do well, good managers will notice and reward their work.

One important management challenge is working with difficult employees.

JOB TEAM

Budget Your Workforce

As a manager, you may need to make a weekly budget. A **budget** is a plan used to decide how money will be spent. To make one, you need to answer some questions. How many hours do you need to fill? Which workers should you use to fill the hours? How much does each worker get paid? How many hours can each employee work?

Look at this example budget and schedule for Hanover Park.

Hanover Park: Park Rangers Weekly Schedule

April 14–20	9AM–1PM	2PM–6PM	Daily Wages
Monday	Leon	Evelyn	$100
Tuesday	Evelyn	Evelyn	$120
Wednesday	Ahmed	Ahmed	$160
Thursday	Ahmed	Ahmed	$160
Friday	Ahmed	Ahmed	$160
Saturday	Ahmed	Ahmed	$160
Sunday	Leon	Ahmed	$120
(Weekly budget: $1,000)		Total Weekly Cost: **$980**	

This schedule shows which shifts each ranger works. It also shows wages paid for each day.

Employees & Wages
Ahmed: $20/hr, FT
Evelyn: $15/hr, PT
Leon: $10/hr, PT

This list tells all the rangers who are available to work. It tells whether they work full or part time and how much they earn.

This shows the budget for a full week of wages. The total weekly cost must be no more than the budget.

1. How many hours does Leon work? _____

2. How many hours does Ahmed work? _____

3. Is this schedule within the park's weekly budget? _____

Hands-Off Management

Work demands often make it difficult for managers to watch every worker. So some managers take a more hands-off approach. This doesn't mean that they give up control. It just means they trust their workers to handle some of the tasks. This gives them time to focus on the work that only they can complete.

As a hands-off manager, you may delegate more work to your employees. This means you will need to train your workers for those tasks. Although you may delegate tasks to others, you will still need a way to check their work. It will be your responsibility that the job is done right.

The manager of a day-care might use a hands-off management style with teachers in different classrooms.

Now suppose you are the manager of an ice cream shop. Use the following information to create a weekly budget for your workers:

- Full-time employees must work between 36 and 40 hours per week.
- Part-time employees can work between 12 and 20 hours per week.
- The store is open from 10 a.m. until 10 p.m. every day.
- The store must have one server and one cashier at all times.
- The total hours per week your employees must cover is 168.
- Your budget for total weekly wages is $1,700.00.

Employees & Wages	
Servers ($10/hour)	**Cashiers ($9/hour)**
Joey (part-time)	Tasha (full-time)
Dana (full-time)	Anthony (part-time)
Francisco (full-time)	Leo (part-time)
	Aiko (part-time)

Using the information, complete the schedule and budget for the week. You should include the following:

- the days and times that employees are scheduled to work
- the total number of hours each employee works
- the total weekly pay that each employee receives
- your weekly labor costs (total weekly pay of all employees)

Use a calculator to total the daily wages.

Complete this schedule:

June 16–22	10AM–2PM	2PM–6PM	6PM–10PM	Daily Wages
Monday	Dana Tasha	Dana Tasha	Francisco Anthony	$228
Tuesday				
Wednesday				
Thursday				
Friday				
Saturday				
Sunday				
(Weekly Budget: $1,700)		Total Weekly Cost: $		

Check off the goals you achieved in Chapter 4.

In Lesson 1, you . . .

☐ Thought about diversity at work

☐ Read examples of discrimination and harassment

☐ Studied discrimination and harassment policies

In Lesson 2, you . . .

☐ Wrote a list of short- and long-term goals

☐ Learned the steps for earning a raise or promotion

☐ Read about how to leave one job and accept another

In Lesson 3, you . . .

☐ Learned the types of education you may need to reach your goals

☐ Read about the ways employers help workers learn new skills

☐ Learned how to update your résumé

In Lesson 4, you . . .

☐ Learned how to promote your successes at work

☐ Learned strategies for shyness

☐ Thought like a supervisor

In Lesson 5, you . . .

☐ Learned how to mentor other employees at work

☐ Studied the responsibilities of a manager

☐ Practiced management skills

What do you want to know more about?

Write the things that you want to learn more about. Talk to your teacher or look them up online.

_____

_____

Choose the best answer.

1. Which of the following is a good example of cultural sensitivity?

    A. asking your co-workers personal questions

    B. laughing about a co-worker's clothing

    C. forwarding humorous e-mails to your co-workers

    D. respecting the religious beliefs of your co-workers

True or false? If the statement is true, write *T*. If the statement is false, write *F*. Then change the false statement to make it true.

2. Most forms of workplace discrimination are easy to spot.

    _____

3. Once people have been hired for a job, they should put their resumes aside until they are ready to look for jobs again.

    _____

Directions: Write your answer to the questions below.

4. How are discrimination and harassment alike? How are they different?

    _____

    _____

    _____

5. Do you think you would make a good manager? Why or why not?

    _____

    _____

    _____

Match the term on the left to the correct definition on the right.

6. intern   A. telling others about your successes

7. promoted   B. moved up to a better position

8. self-promotion   C. to give responsibility to someone

9. delegate   D. giving someone a good reason to want to do something

10. motivation   E. a student who works at a job to get experience

GLOSSARY

budget a plan for how to spend money

certificate a document that proves that you have trained for a skill

compromise a way to reach an agreement in which each person or group gives up something

conduct the way you behave; your behavior

co-pay payment you must make each time you get medical care

corporate culture the values and behavior of the people in a company

corporate structure the way in which a company's jobs and departments are organized

cost-of-living raise a small raise in pay that helps workers to pay for basic needs

coverage the amount or type of protection given by an insurance plan

cultural sensitivity an awareness of the various backgrounds of others

customer a person or a group who buys goods or uses services from a business

customer service the help that a company gives to the people who buy its products or use its services

deductible the amount you must pay before insurance begins to cover your expenses

delegate give control or responsibility to someone

direct reports employees who work for a supervisor

disciplinary action a process used to correct an employee who breaks work rules

discrimination unfair treatment of a person or group of people

diverse made up of things or people that are different from each other

ethnicity group of people with the same customs, language, religion, etc.

feedback helpful information that is given to show what can be done to improve something

gender a person's sex, either male or female

generation a group of people born and living during the same time

gross pay your pay before taxes and deductions are taken out

group dynamic how people act in a group

harassment conduct meant to disturb or upset another employee

hazard danger; something that can cause harm

human resources the department in a company that deals with hiring, training, and other employee issues

incentive something that encourages a person to work harder

intern a student who works at a job to get experience

lingo the special terms used by a group of people

mentor a more experienced employee who helps train a new worker

merit raise a raise in pay a worker earns because of outstanding job performance

motivation giving someone a good reason to want to do something

net pay your pay after taxes and deductions are taken out

networking building relationships with other people to help your career

payroll deductions money taken from your paycheck for things like retirement savings and health insurance

policies the rules a company makes to keep work going well and safely

procedure the steps you follow in order to do something.

promotion a move up to a better position

résumé a short document describing your education, work history, and skills

retire to end a job or career

self-awareness knowing your own personality

self-discipline the ability to make yourself do things that need to be done

self-esteem a feeling of pride and confidence in yourself

self-promotion telling others about your skills and successes

shift the time you are scheduled to work

stress mental pressure or worry

stressors events that cause stress

support staff workers who help other employees do their work

technology the use of science to solve problems or invent useful things; sometimes called *tech*

wage the amount of money a worker is paid

Chapter 1

Page 8, Job Math

1. $400.00, $800.00, $20,800.00
2. $349.50, $699.00, $18,174.00

Page 9, Learn Your Way Around

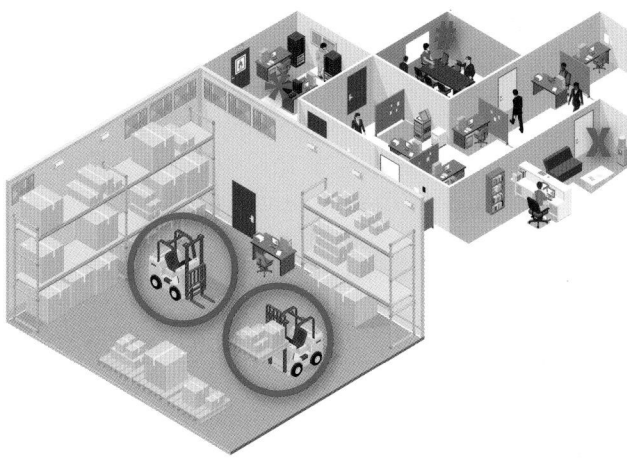

Page 10, Read Work Schedules

1. 21 hours
2. Hanh
3. Reynaldo
4. Olivia
5. 7pm-10pm
6. 8 hours
7. Skylar
8. April 5-11

Page 14, Understand Workplace Policies

1. No, an employee cannot have a gun on company property.
2. *Possible answers:* bullying, inappropriate language, offensive comments, sexual talk, yelling, abusive language
3. At the rate of one day per month, Jamal would earn four days of vacation.

Page 19, Health Care Plan A or B?

Answers will vary. Students should include reasons why they chose A or B.

Page 21, Understand Training Manuals

Answers will vary.

Page 22, Safety Warnings

Answers will vary.

Page 29, Analyze GIS Data

1. There are areas where there is potential gold.
2. Near the limestone deposit: area G.
3. Yes, there are areas with kaolin.
4. Fuller's earth

Page 31, Cultural Clues

A. Employees celebrate co-workers' birthdays.
B. Co-workers are encouraged to attend events. They may get free tickets to sporting events or performances.
C. A group of co-workers attends happy hour at a local bar after work.
D. Employees are allowed to wear headphones and listen to music while they work.

Page 33, Where Do You Fit In?

1. *Possible answers:* I would read the materials provided by the employer that explain parts of the corporate culture; I would watch my co-workers; I would ask questions of my co-workers.
2. *Possible answer:* I would feel comfortable taking a turn to buy donuts for my co-workers on Friday. It would be a good way to build friendship with my co-workers. There would also be little risk of upsetting or offending anyone.
3. *Possible answer:* I would not feel comfortable going to happy hour. While it could be fun to hang out with co-workers, I would prefer to avoid activities in which employees are drinking alcohol.

Page 35, Chapter Review

1. B
2. F: For each dependent you claim on your W-4 form, the government withholds <u>less</u> money from your paycheck.
3. T

4. Employees can learn about corporate culture by looking at the values and behaviors of people at the company.

5. C

6. F

7. B

8. A

9. D

10. E

Chapter 2

Page 37, Professional Behaviors

Circle the following behaviors: talking with a co-worker about a work task, folding clothes, and helping a customer at the cash register.

Draw an X over the following behaviors: texting during work hours, wearing clothes you would wear to a nightclub, and arriving late to work.

Page 38, Personal or Professional?

1. Professional

2. Personal

3. Personal

Page 41, The Group Dynamic

Answers will vary.

Page 43, Work on Your Own

Answers will vary.

Page 45, Leadership Styles

Answers will vary.

Follow-up: Possible examples of good leadership include honest, competent, plans for the future, intelligent, inspiring, imaginative, enthusiastic, straightforward, confident, fair-minded, analytical, and committed to excellence. Possible examples of poor leadership: impatient, aggressive, dishonest, incompetent, poor character, poor communication skills, self-serving, one-size-fits-all thinking, lack of focus and follow through, not planning for the future, and not customer focused.

Page 47, Conflict Resolution

Scene 1: Possible answer: Sabeen should agree to not make personal calls while at work. Tanya should promise to be honest with her supervisors about Sabeen's job performance.

Scene 2: Possible answer: James and Mick should work together because both have something to offer the company. James should respect Mick's views because Mick knows the latest technology. Mick should respect James' views because James has a lot of practical experience.

Scene 3: Possible answer: Carlos and Suzanne need to behave like professionals. They need to understand how their behavior affects the others in the department as well as their chances of being promoted. If one of them is promoted to head the department, then the other should respect that decision and behave like a professional.

Page 48, Be the Supervisor

The supervisor should give both servers a chance to tell their sides of the conflict. The supervisor should only address behaviors and not allow the employees to bring personal feelings into the conflict. Both servers should have the chance to suggest a compromise.

Page 53, The Unhappy Customer

The server should listen to the customer's complaint about being overcharged. The server should ask questions, apologize, and offer a solution. The goal was for the customer to feel satisfied and to want to eat at the restaurant in the future.

Page 54, The Needy Patient

The LPN should listen to the patient's concern, and then explain his/her other work duties. The LPN should let the patient know he/she will return as soon as the other duties are taken care of.

Page 54, Taking an Order

The gardener should listen to the park manager's needs, ask questions, and take careful notes. The gardener should read his/her notes to the manager to be sure he/she had gotten the order right. The manager should clearly provide the order information to the gardener. He/she should also ask questions and restate to ensure the order is correct.

Page 55, Calculate Percentages

1. $3
2. $7
3. $3,888.00

Page 56, What Are Your Stressors?

Honestly tell some things that cause stress in your daily life and how you deal with them. Then ask your teacher to look at your answer and give you feedback.

Page 61, Chapter Review

1. B
2. F: Working independently requires <u>more</u> self-discipline than working in a group.
3. T
4. *Sample answer:* It's important to be professional because your conduct may be judged even when you're not at work.
5. C
6. A
7. F
8. E
9. B
10. D

Chapter 3

Page 62, Be Your Own Cheerleader

Answers will vary.

Page 69, Now You Try It

Sample answer: Angie could say, "I don't mind working on my day off for an important reason. What I need to know is why we are taking this rush job. As part of the team, I'd like to know all of the facts."

Pages 70–71, Office Gossip and Accept Feedback

Answers will vary.

Page 75, Know the Terms

Answers will vary.

Page 77, Chapter Review

1. A
2. B
3. C
4. T
5. F: Performance reviews can sometimes affect workers' wages or salaries.
6. Be professional and focus on job performance. Don't let your personal feelings affect your judgment.
7. D
8. A
9. C
10. B

Chapter 4

Page 79, Working Together

Answers will vary.

Page 81, Discrimination Policy

1. An equal opportunity employer does not discriminate against its employees or the people it might hire.
2. No; a manager in this company would not be allowed to promote a person based on his or her race.
3. Employees cannot discriminate, either positively or negatively, based on race, ethnicity, religion, sexual preference, or gender.

Page 83, Harassment Policy

1. This company takes harassment very seriously and has many possible ways to correct it.
2. This company may address harassment through training, sending employees to a counselor, and/or disciplinary action.
3. This company would look into what had happened. Then, depending on how serious the offense was, they would choose how to correct it.

Page 85, What Are Your Goals?

Answers will vary.

Page 89, How to Reach Your Goals

Answers will vary.

Page 93, Me in 10 Years

Your answer should include some short-term goals that lead to the 10-year goal you wrote on page 89. Your list should include all the possible costs (such as time and money) for reaching the goals.

Page 97, Self-Promotion

Circle the following statements: "I am so excited! I got a perfect score on my training test!" and "I just opened my fifth credit account of the day!"

Draw an X over the following statements: "Good thing I was at the meeting because Jessie really messed up." and "Hi, Felicia! Did you see I beat your sales record?"

Page 97, Hey, Look at Me!

You should honestly rate the ideas for self-promotion that are given and the ones you add. Your personal plan should list the ways that will work best for you.

Page 98, Just a Note

Your note should list your classroom successes for the week.

Page 100, Who Are Your Mentors?

Your first list should include the people who have acted as your mentors and how they helped you. Your second list should include the ways you have acted as a mentor to others.

Page 102, Be the Manager

Your plan should include all lessons, supplies, and equipment the class needs for the week.

Pages 104–105, Budget Your Workforce

Your budget should

- stay within the weekly wage budget

- cover all the work hours
- schedule full-time workers for 36-40 hours

Sample schedule:

June 16–22	10AM–2PM	2PM–6PM	6PM–10PM	Daily Wages
Monday	Dana Tasha	Dana Tasha	Francisco Anthony	$228
Tuesday	Dana Tasha	Dana Tasha	Francisco Anthony	$228
Wednesday	Dana Tasha	Dana Tasha	Francisco Anthony	$228
Thursday	Dana Tasha	Dana Tasha	Joey Anthony	$228
Friday	Dana Tasha	Francisco Leo	Francisco Leo	$228
Saturday	Joey Aiko	Francisco Aiko	Francisco Leo	$228
Sunday	Joey Aiko	Francisco Aiko	Francisco Leo	$228
(Weekly Budget: $1,700)			Total Weekly Cost: $1,596	

Page 107, Chapter Review

1. D
2. T
3. F: Once you have been hired for a job, you should <u>keep your résumé up to date</u>.
4. They can both harm workers. They may also be caused by the same things. For example, you can be harassed or discriminated against based on your religion.
5. Accept reasonable answers.
6. E
7. B
8. A
9. C
10. D